THE
ABC'S
OF
WISDOM

THE

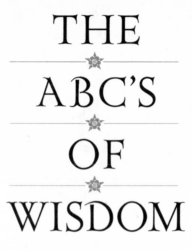

ABC'S

OF

WISDOM

Building Character
with Solomon

RAY
PRITCHARD

MOODY PRESS
CHICAGO

ISBN: 0-8024-8182-5

1 3 5 7 9 10 8 6 4 2

Printed in the United States of America

CONTENTS

ACKNOWLEDGMENTS

Phyllis Raad, Sherrie Puknaitis, Rebecca Arellanes, Mia Gale, Kathy Duggins, and her daughters Sarah and Katie all contributed in various ways to the writing of this book. I have gained valuable insight from Craig Steiner, Larry Korbus, Bob Boerman, and Davis Duggins. Greg Thornton of Moody Press gave me constant encouragement, as did Julie-Allyson Ieron, Suzanne Dowd, Jim Bell, and my very gifted editor, Anne Scherich. I am also indebted to Sherry Flipps for her prayers. Special thanks to my wife, Marlene, and to my three sons, Joshua, Mark, and Nicholas, for teaching me most of the important things I have learned in life.

INTRODUCTION

Almost everyone agrees that we are living in a day of moral and cultural confusion. Former Secretary of Education William Bennett says that it is almost as if our society has conspired to make it impossible for our children to grow up as decent, moral individuals. He argues that if we want to improve our nation, we must once again dedicate ourselves to the hard work of inculcating virtue in the lives of our children. We must teach them about things like justice, humility, honesty, hard work, thrift, self-control, kindness, and perseverance.

But William Bennett is not the only one saying these things. *Newsweek* magazine recently published a cover story titled "The New Virtue-Crats." The lead article reported that 76 percent of all Americans surveyed agree that our nation is in a serious moral and spiritual decline. Although we can argue about *why* it happened or even about *how* it happened, the fact itself seems to be beyond debate. Somewhere, somehow, we as a people lost the concept of character and virtue.

Chuck Colson argues that for the first time in our history we have raised an entire generation of young people who have no conscience. Since their parents had solid moral foundation, they had nothing to pass a to their children. As a result, many young people today do not know the difference between right and wrong.

As a result of losing the concept of absolute standards, we have entered what *Newsweek* calls "the age of enlightenment skepticism," where it's OK for you, but not OK for me; it's right for you, but not right for me; wrong for you, but not wrong for me; you've got your way and I've got my way. But if there are no absolute standards, then dishonesty is just as good as honesty, hatred is just as noble as compassion, and laziness is as commendable as hard work.

If America is going to change, the hearts of people have to change one by one. That can only happen as Christians begin to live by moral standards that truly are not of this world. As we face an increasingly skeptical society, we must consciously demonstrate a superior kind of ethical behavior, for we can preach all we want, but until others see the difference incarnated in us, it will be all talk, just another Sunday morning sermon.

All that I have written so far may sound rather gloomy—and indeed there are dark clouds on the national horizon. But here is where the good news begins. If virtue is what we need, then I know where we can go to find it. Three thousand years ago the wisest man who ~~r~~ lived (with the exception of Jesus Himself) wrote the fundamental principles of moral behavior that formed Jewish and Christian thinking ever since. those truths laid the foundation for what we ay as Western civilization.

I am speaking of the ancient book of Proverbs. King Solomon wrote most of the book. It was evidently intended to be an ancient *Book of Virtues* for the young people of his day. It represents the distilled wisdom of the ages. His sentences are direct and to the point. He never uses three words when two will do. He doesn't preach in the normal sense of that word, nor does he threaten. In hundreds of pithy sayings he sets forth the basic principles of moral behavior.

In this book we are going to take a look at one hundred areas of moral and spiritual concern. You should know right up front that this is not a commentary on Proverbs. It is instead a practical handbook for virtuous living based on the sayings of Solomon.

One final note and we're ready to begin. Please don't feel compelled to read this book straight through. Actually, I hope you won't do that. You'll get the greatest benefit from reading one section at a time and pondering the questions at the end. The sections are arranged alphabetically to make it easy to find the topics of greatest interest to you.

This book is not really about children or even for children. But I do believe that the up-and-coming generation needs to heed these words. For that matter, we could all benefit from some practical, down-to-earth teaching about what is right and what is wrong and how to treat the people we meet every day.

For a world that has lost its way, God wrote a book to bring us back to reality. If you're interested in learnin how life is supposed to work, turn the page, and let's get started.

Great class for session

ACCOUNTABILITY

---❖---

How to Reach Your Full Potential

As iron sharpens iron, so one man sharpens another.
Proverbs 27:17

Anyone who has ever owned a knife understands this proverb. When iron becomes blunt, another piece of iron is used to sharpen it. That process necessarily involves heat, friction, and very close contact. You can't sharpen an ax from a distance. You have to get close enough to make the sparks fly.

Even so, one man may "sharpen" another, but you have to get close enough to let the sparks fly. That implies openness, honesty, vulnerability, and the willingness to receive constructive criticism.

Howard Hendricks says that every man needs a Paul, a Barnabas, and a Timothy. *Paul* represents that person in your life to whom you look for spiritual leadership. He (or she) is that person who keeps urging you to "press toward the mark" of God's high calling in your life. This person could be a husband or a wife. More often it will be a close friend or a co-worker; very often it might be an older person you greatly admire. Your "Paul" is that one key person you look to when things begin to fall apart, when your back is against the wall, when you find yourself confused about the next step you should take. You'll grow faster if you've got someone around you who can give you good counsel when you really need it.

Barnabas represents that person in your life who is probably your best friend. He (or she) is a friend who sticks closer than a brother. You may not get much advice from this friend (except indirectly), but your "Barnabas" is that person who brightens your life by his very presence. Your "Barnabas" could be a husband or wife, but often will be a very close friend who can weep over your defeats and cheer your victories. This person is a true "Son of Encouragement" to you, lightening your load simply by being there for you. We all need a "Barnabas," for life is tough enough as it is.

Timothy represents that person in your life to whom you are a "Paul." He (or she) may be a new believer or a younger Christian. He (or she) will be a person in whom you sense great potential for Jesus Christ. As you spend time together, you share your heart, your understanding of God, your daily walk with Christ. You let this person get close enough to see you, warts and all. Why? So that you can develop your "Timothy" into a strong soldier for Jesus Christ. This may be done in a formal way, by meeting weekly for prayer and Bible study. Or it may happen as you check in with each other to see how things are going. You need a "Timothy" in your life so that all the things God is teaching you don't stop with you.

So . . .

Who is your "Paul"?

Who is your "Barnabas"?

Who is your "Timothy"?

You need a mentor, you need a close friend, and you need someone who looks up to you for guidance. Or to say it another way, follow Paul, be a Barnabas, find a Timothy.

Lord, I see too many blunt edges in my life. Sharpen me that I might be a useful tool in Your hands. Amen.

How do you answer the three questions above?

Who is currently holding you accountable for your own spiritual growth? If the answer is "no one," what do you plan to do about it?

AFFIRMATION

❖

Finding Something Good to Say

An anxious heart weighs a man down, but a kind word cheers him up.

Proverbs 12:25

Proverbs has much to say about the importance of affirmation. "The tongue that brings healing is a tree of life" (15:4a). "The mouth of the righteous is a fountain of life" (10:11a). "A man finds joy in giving an apt reply—and how good is a timely word!" (15:23). "Pleasant words are a honeycomb, sweet to the soul and healing to the bones" (16:24).

For many years, Henrietta Mears was director of Christian education at Hollywood Presbyterian Church. God gave her a wonderful insight into human nature. These are her words: "Whenever I meet a new person, I imagine them wearing a sign across their chest which reads, 'My name is _____. Please help me feel important.'" Helping people feel important is what affirmation is all about.

But where should we begin? I have three suggestions:

First, make sure you begin each day by saying an encouraging word to each member of your family. Have you ever had one of those "uh-huh" breakfasts? That's what happens when you are too frazzled to talk intelligently to each other. So you grunt. "Would you like some coffee, sweetheart?" "Uh-huh." "Don't forget your lunch." "Uh-huh." "Where's my geometry book?" "Uh-huh." "Can I borrow a hundred dollars, Dad?" "Uh-huh." "Would you like a dead rat with your scrambled eggs?" "Uh-huh."

We've all had mornings like that. Just make sure it doesn't become a habit. Take time to encourage each other before you go out the door.

Second, before you say a word of criticism, say a prayer for the person you are criticizing. This is simply a practical piece of advice. If we criticize without praying, we run the risk of speaking in anger and saying things we regret later. But if we pray first, the venom is drained out of our words. We may even lose our anger completely and decide that the criticism is unwarranted.

Third, when you feel the slightest urge to encourage someone, go ahead and do it. Make a simple resolution that every time you feel like encouraging someone this week, you will go ahead and do it. Just put aside your work, get up from your desk, pick up the phone, write a note, pat someone on the back, say a good word to lift someone's spirits. Try doing it for just one week. Who knows? It might become a permanent habit.

The story is told of a little second-grade boy who was trying out for a part in the school play. The day came for the auditions and his mother took him to school and waited for him to come out. She was nervous because she knew he couldn't sing, couldn't act, and couldn't memorize very well. So she was surprised when he came out

21

after forty-five minutes with a big smile on his face. "How did it go, honey?" "It was great, Mom. Guess what? I've been chosen to clap and cheer."

In truth, that could be said about all of us. We have all been chosen by God to clap and cheer for our brothers and sisters in Jesus Christ. They need to hear it and we need to do it. Let the applause begin.

Father, make me a messenger of hope and encouragement to those I meet today. Amen.

Whom do you know who needs a word of encouragement right now?

Did you come from an encouraging family? How would you rate your own family in this area? What can you do to make things more positive?

ANGER

❖

A Warning for Hotheads

An angry man stirs up dissension, and a hot-tempered one commits many sins.

Proverbs 29:22

Here is a simple fact: *Either you learn to control your temper or your temper will control you.* How many of us have undergone tremendous heartache because at a crucial moment we lost our temper and spouted off when we should have been silent?

We all know that anger is a powerful emotion that can be used for good or for evil. *Anger isn't always wrong.* We know, for instance, that anger is one of the attributes of God. Did you know that the Bible speaks over a hundred times of the anger of God? We know that God never sins, yet the Bible speaks repeatedly of His anger toward sin and disobedience. We know also that there are times when anger is justified and even righteous. Ephesians 4:26 says, "In your anger do not sin."

When we see people hurting other people, when we watch the wholesale slaughter of the unborn, when we see children being lured into drugs and prostitution, when we see families torn apart by sin, *that ought to make us angry.* If we sit idly by while the world goes to hell, if we don't get angry, if we don't weep, if we don't care, then something is wrong deep inside us.

So then, anger can be a very useful and even Christian emotion. *However, righteous anger can quickly lead us in the wrong direction.* The same verse that says, "In your anger do not sin," adds this phrase, "Do not let the sun go down while you are still angry." That is, don't go to bed angry. Even if your anger is justified, don't go to sleep that way. Deal with it, talk it out, pray it out, walk it out—but don't try to sleep it out. That won't work.

What happens when you don't deal with your anger? It settles deep in your heart, it hardens like concrete, it distorts your personality, it squeezes out your joy, it oozes the smelly black gunk of unhappiness over every part of your life. That's why the very next verse in Ephesians offers this warning: "Do not give the devil a foothold" (Ephesians 4:27).

All rock climbers understand that verse. In order to get up the side of the mountain, you've got to get a firm foothold. *That's what Satan wants to do in your life—he wants to use your anger (even your legitimate anger) to get a foothold in your heart.*

The first step is admitting you have a problem. So many of us have a public face that looks good and a private face we keep behind locked gates and stone walls, a face of anger and hatred.

Next, share your struggles with a trusted friend. If you have someone who will hold you accountable, you're much less likely to say or do something foolish.

Third, ask the Lord Jesus to give specific help in the area of your anger. Name the sin, confess it, and claim the power of the indwelling Christ.

Jesus has shown us the way. You don't have to live in anger and bitterness over the way people treat you. Through the power of the Holy Spirit your life can be different.

Lord Jesus, thank you for showing us how to live. May Your love replace any anger in my heart. Amen.

When was the last time you got angry? What happened? Are you satisfied with the way you handled the situation?

What are your own personal warning signs that you have crossed the line from righteous to unrighteous anger?

BEAUTY

—❋—

Enjoy It, but Don't Bank on It

Charm is deceptive, and beauty is fleeting; but a woman who fears the Lord is to be praised.

Proverbs 31:30

If you had the power to change your body, would you use it? Suppose you could instantly change the way you look. Would you do it? For most of us the question is not, Would you use that power? but rather, Would it be a simple repair or a complete makeover? Would you say, "Lord, let's just start all over again"? Would we even recognize you?

Our bodies wear out, they sag, they expand, they wrinkle, the joints get creaky, the arteries harden, the heart slows down, the eyes grow dim, the teeth fall out, the back is stooped, the arms grow weary. Our bones break, our muscles weaken. The body bulges in the wrong places. It happens to all of us sooner or later.

There is coming a day when your body won't need changing. You won't grow old and you won't get cancer. *Jesus Christ will give you a brand-new body.* Until then, we live in hope, waiting patiently for that day to come.

That perspective explains so much that happens to us. God is weaning you away from putting your hope in the things of this world so that your hope will be in Him alone. The only way He can wean you away from the things of this world is through suffering and difficulty. He brings you to the place where you must say, "Lord, it's You and You alone." He's teaching you to wait on Him. Right now you're trying to scheme your way into a better situation. But eventually you'll say, "Lord, if it takes forever, go ahead. Take Your time. My hope is in You."

None of this should suggest that beauty is useless. It is, however, "fleeting" and can be misleading. Both Saul and David were handsome men, yet one man came to a very bad end while the other, though not perfect, was a man after God's own heart. Beauty is not only in the eye of the beholder, it is also only skin deep. Beauty is fine, but character is better. The only other reference to beauty in Proverbs comes as a warning about the immoral woman in 6:25: "Do not lust in your heart after her beauty or let her captivate you with her eyes." Likewise, the only New Testament references to human beauty speak of "the unfading beauty of a gentle and quiet spirit" (1 Peter 3:4).

Note also that "charm is deceptive." The word *charm* carries with it the idea of being attractive, fascinating, and slightly mysterious. This is not a warning against good manners and good grooming, but against relying on outward appearance to gain favor with others. Such a person relies on good looks, a nice wardrobe, a knowing laugh, a radiant smile, and general self-confidence to carry him wherever he wants to go.

Against all this we have the simple statement that "a

woman who fears the Lord is to be praised." Because she has relied on the Lord all her life, she is more beautiful at the end than at the beginning. Her beauty will never fade because it comes from the inside out.

Lord, may I have the inner beauty that comes from knowing You. Amen.

If you could change anything about the way you look, what would it be?

Which do you think about more—the state of your soul or the state of your wardrobe? What steps have you taken recently to improve your "inner beauty"?

BOASTING

❖

The Loud Sound of an Empty Mind

Do not boast about tomorrow, for you do not know what a day may bring forth.

Proverbs 27:1

This is one of the most famous verses in the book of Proverbs and one of the most often quoted. In tones that are darkly ominous, it reminds us of a truth no one can escape. Life *is* uncertain. No one knows what tomorrow will bring.

Think of what you would know if you knew the future. You could invest in the stock market and make money every time. You could pass every test because you would know the questions in advance. You would never be surprised by a sudden snowstorm or an unexpected visitor. Every business plan would succeed because you would have perfectly planned for every contingency. Nervous suitors would never pop the question until they knew in advance the answer would be yes.

There are at least three reasons it is good that you don't know your future. *Number one, if you knew the future, you wouldn't be able to understand it.* So many factors play into what is going to happen six months from now that we couldn't comprehend them all. Most of us want simple answers: "Will the stock market go up or down?"

"Should I take that new job?" "If I ask Jill to marry me, will she say yes?" God says, "I can't really answer it that way. I have to show you the big picture." But if He showed us the big picture, we wouldn't understand it.

Number two, if you knew the future, it would make you either lazy or arrogant. Someone has said that luck is what happens when preparation meets opportunity. It's true that hard work doesn't guarantee success. But hard work creates the climate in which success is more likely to take place. One reason we work hard is precisely because we *don't* know the future. If you knew how the stock market was going to do next year, it might tend to make you take it easy. Why work hard when you already know what tomorrow will bring? That same knowledge might tend to make you arrogant because you would be privy to inside information. Either way—whether lazy or arrogant—you wouldn't be a very nice person to be around.

Number three, knowing your personal future would eventually lead to despair. Suppose someone handed you a manila envelope and told you it contained a detailed account of your next ten years. Would you open it? The temptation would be almost irresistible. But suppose the envelope contained news of a forthcoming tragedy that you could not avoid. Knowing the future would then be a curse, not a blessing. We think we want to know the future, but really we don't. It's better not to know, for then we're forced to take life as it comes—moment by moment, hour by hour, day by day.

Boasting is foolish because it makes us think we control the future when we don't even control the present. At its heart boasting is a subtle form of idolatry in which we attempt to push God off the throne.

If you want to boast, boast that you know the Lord. That's the only thing that matters. And leave the future in God's hands. He can handle it just fine by Himself.

Lord, when I am tempted to boast about my plans, please remind me that You can run the universe without any help from me. Amen.

Suppose you were given the opportunity to discover the next ten years of your life in advance. Would you take that opportunity? Why or why not?

If you could know just one fact about your own personal future, what would it be? How would knowing that fact change the way you live today?

What is the essential difference between making wise plans and boasting about the future?

BORROWING

---❖---

It's Not Wrong, but It Can Be Dangerous

The rich rule over the poor, and the borrower is servant to the lender.

Proverbs 22:7

No one should be surprised that Solomon has so much to say about money. After all, we live in a world where money is the measure of all things. Like it or not, we are evaluated by how much we make, how much we spend, and how conspicuously we spend it. The currency of the day is the credit card. Who among us goes shopping without at least one credit card—for identification, if not to make our purchases?

But the problem is deeper than those little rectangles of plastic. Over and over Proverbs warns us of the danger of making money the measure of life. "Do not wear yourself out to get rich; have the wisdom to show restraint. Cast but a glance at riches, and they are gone, for they will surely sprout wings and fly off to the sky like an eagle" (23:4–5). Those who are in a hurry to get money find that once they get it, it has a way of slipping through their fingers.

Take your time, Solomon says. Work hard, save your money, don't buy what you can't afford. Remember that wealth in any amount is a gift from God. Be honest in all your dealings; don't rig the scales to gain an advantage. Beware of bribes, don't oppress the poor, and be generous, and God will be generous to you. These tried-and-true principles are the secrets of financial freedom.

It is against that backdrop that we should consider Proverbs 22:7. The first half makes an observation on the way of the world that cannot be denied. As the saying goes, money talks. This is not a moral judgment but a simple fact of life. It is the world's version of the Golden Rule: Those who have the gold make the rules. But the second half is equally important. In what way is the borrower a servant to the lender? He is a servant because the lender has a legal (and moral) claim on his money. If he defaults, the lender can (and often does) take him to court, where he may lose all his possessions. All that he has is at risk until the loan is paid off.

Does this mean it is wrong to borrow money? No. Solomon simply intends to remind us that there is no such thing as a "free" loan. If it's "free," it's not a loan; if it's a loan, it's not "free."

Far too many people have a cavalier attitude toward debt, which is why they run up credit card bills into the tens of thousands of dollars. But at that point, they are in prison, whether they know it or not. And because of their careless actions, they aren't free to be generous to others and to the Lord. In the words of Harry Ironside, "It is far better to be in meager circumstances and dependent on God, than to have plenty but to know it belongs to another." He goes on to say that Christians should fear debt and flee from it—an injunction that sounds odd to our ears but one which Solomon would no doubt have approved.

Before you take out a loan, remember that the lender is on top and you are on the bottom. If you can't make the payments, don't take the loan. It's as simple as that.

Lord Jesus, when I am tempted to live beyond my means, remind me that You owned nothing but the clothes on Your back. Amen.

How much money would it take to get you completely out of debt right now? Would you be embarrassed for your friends to know the answer to that question? If the answer is yes, what steps should you be taking to get out of debt?

BRIBERY

❋

A Fast Train to Destruction

A greedy man brings trouble to his family, but he who hates bribes will live.

Proverbs 15:27

Solomon had a lot to say about this subject, nearly all of it negative. For instance, an adulterer cannot bribe his way out of punishment (6:35). Bribery perverts the course of justice (17:23). A leader who seeks bribes destroys his own country (29:4). Bribery is a form of greed that eventually hurts a man and his family (15:27).

Two other verses must also be considered. "A bribe is a charm to the one who gives it; wherever he turns, he succeeds" (17:8). "A gift given in secret soothes anger, and a bribe concealed in the cloak pacifies great wrath" (21:14). Is Solomon contradicting himself? Not at all. These two verses simply state facts, not moral judgments. Bribery often works, which is why it happens so often. Many people have risen to high position by offering money or other favors in exchange for the help they need. In the second verse, the "gift given in secret" is not necessarily a bribe. It may simply be an attempt to turn away anger by the offering of a gift.

Why is bribery so destructive? Because it is based on a shortsighted view of the moral universe. When individuals feel they must take matters into their own hands, they are implicitly denying that God can take care of them. They break the rules because they doubt the goodness of God. For them, money (or power or position or some other reward) has become an idol that has displaced the Lord.

Proverbs 16:8 says, "Better a little with righteousness than much gain with injustice." That is to say, it is better to do right and struggle than to do wrong and be rich. Better to follow the rules and go broke than to cheat and climb your way to what you think is the top of the ladder. It is better to struggle to make ends meet, knowing that you are righteous in the eyes of God, than to cheat other people to have it all.

Proverbs 15:16 adds: "Better a little with the fear of the Lord than great wealth with turmoil." Too many people have bought into the notion that money brings happiness. We think that if we only had another $1,000 or $5,000 or $10,000 or $50,000 or $150,000, then, at last, we would be able to buy that thing we have been trying to buy, or we'd be able to move up to a newer house or better car or better part of the country. The Bible is not against wealth or prosperity, but it is very honest about it. Generally speaking, the people who have lots of money also have a lot of trouble.

It is precisely because men don't believe that sentence that they turn to bribery. We cheat because we don't trust God and because we have made worldly gain our goal in life.

Bribery is truly a fast train to destruction. Stay away

from it. Don't take bribes. Don't offer bribes. Play by the rules. And let God take care of the results.

> *Lord, save me from the impatience of greed and the stupidity of breaking the rules to get ahead. Amen.*

What is the essential difference between a sinful bribe and a legitimate gift?

How much money would it take to make you happy right now?

CAUTION

Look Before You Leap

It is not good to have zeal without knowledge, nor to be hasty and miss the way.

Proverbs 19:2

What you have seen with your eyes do not bring hastily to court, for what will you do in the end if your neighbor puts you to shame?

Proverbs 25:8

The key word in both verses is *hasty.* Zeal for God by itself is a noble quality. A zealous person is one who has made a commitment to a particular course of action and, having made that commitment, bends all his energies to carry it out. In a passage made famous by Handel's *Messiah,* Isaiah speaks of the great things the Lord Jesus will accomplish by His coming to the earth. He will establish His kingdom, ruling over the entire earth from David's throne in Jerusalem. That great future, yet future to us, will happen because "the zeal of the Lord Almighty will accomplish this" (Isaiah 9:7c). God has spoken it, and, at the right moment, He will bring all His divine energy to bear to bring it to pass.

But Solomon warns us about "zeal without knowledge." What does he mean? God's zeal is guided by His perfect knowledge of all things. Because we do not have the luxury of perfect knowledge, we often face the temptation of acting too fast or speaking too soon.

The meaning is clear: Don't open your mouth until you have something to say. Get all the facts, get them straight, think things through, and then take action. But what if you think your neighbor has cheated you? Should we simply let others take advantage of us? The answer, of course, is no. Solomon isn't suggesting that we become punching bags for the neighborhood bully.

Just remember, though, that there are always two sides to a story. In fact, there are at least two and sometimes more sides—"my side, your side, and the right side." Just because you think you're right doesn't mean you are. Or at least it doesn't mean the judge will see it your way.

These are wise words in this litigious age where even Christians are quick to threaten lawsuits against those who have wronged them. It ought to be difficult for a believer to say "I'll sue you," especially to another believer (*see* 1 Corinthians 6:1–8). You may end up losing everything—the case, your money, and your reputation.

Take your time. Get the facts. Don't be quick to pass judgment. You don't have to answer every question or pursue every grievance against you. It has been well said that God gave us two ears and one mouth so that we would listen twice as much as we talk. That's good advice for all of us, especially for those who talk first and listen later.

Zeal is good, but zeal without knowledge can get you in a heap of trouble.

Lord, give me the wisdom to know when to take action and the courage to wait until the time is right. Amen.

When was the last time you made a major decision you later regretted? Looking back, how could you have avoided making that mistake?

What are the current major issues in your life? Which ones need more study before making a decision?

CHARACTER

❖

More Precious than Gold

*A good name is more desirable than great riches; to be es-
teemed is better than silver or gold.*

Proverbs 22:1

Of all the gifts we can give to our children, none is
greater than the gift of a good name. In the small
town in Alabama where I grew up, my father was a well-
known and greatly loved physician. There were four of us
Pritchard boys who grew up in that small town. Outside
our circle of friends we were known as "Dr. Pritchard's
sons." In those days, that meant a certain responsibility
was laid on our shoulders. We had to live up to the good
name our father had established. And we knew—boy, did
we know!—that if we ever got into trouble our misbehav-
ior would reflect badly on our father.

My father has been dead for many years. But when I
go back to visit that small town, someone always recog-
nizes me as "Dr. Pritchard's son." Such is the power of a
good name; such is the enduring relationship that lasts
long after a father has died. And to be truthful, the sweet-
est, most wonderful compliment anyone can ever pay to
me is to say, "Your father would be proud of you." He
had a good name, a name that has lasted longer than his
own life. When I teach my boys about their grandfather, I

am passing that good name down to the next generation.

I find it interesting that Solomon makes a comparison between riches and a good name. Money is good, but how others esteem you is much more important. What will you have to show for your life when it is over? What legacy will you leave behind?

What good will money do you after you are dead? You can't spend it, you can't invest it, you can't even give it away. The same goes for all that money can buy—stocks and bonds, a business, a college degree, a nice home, two cars in the garage, a summer home in the country. They all stay behind when you die.

Most of what you work for will be left behind when they lower you into the ground. Your money is no big deal. Somebody else gets it after you're gone. Your position at work? It's filled before the funeral. Your degrees, your awards, your prized possessions? Nice stuff, but it's gathering dust in the attic.

Is there anything at all that you can take with you when you die? I can think of two things, but they have nothing to do with money.

One is *character;* the other, *relationships.* After you are gone, we'll remember two things about you: what kind of person you were and how you treated people. God says, "Live your life any way you want. But when it's over, only two things will remain for eternity—your character and your relationships. The rest goes up in smoke."

Lord, help me to focus on the things that really matter, so that when the smoke clears, I'll have something to show for my life on earth. Amen.

What kind of "name" did you inherit from your parents?

If you have children, what kind of "name" are you leaving them?

Why is a good name more important than silver or gold?

CHEERFULNESS

---❖---

The Healing Power of a Merry Heart

A cheerful heart is good medicine, but a crushed spirit dries up the bones.

Proverbs 17:22

Doctors have known for a long time that there is a close relationship between the physical and the spiritual sides of life. Even though the precise relationship is difficult to define or to quantify, every doctor has seen the principle in action. Ask any doctor and he or she will give you dozens of stories of patients who should have died but didn't—and the only possible explanation was their positive, hope-filled outlook on life. Ask that same doctor, and he or she will give you another dozen stories of people who came into treatment in a negative or angry or hostile mode and who stayed sicker longer than they should have. And every doctor has seen cases where a person died even though he should have gotten better. In many of those instances, the patient seemed to just give up. And once he gave up, he died.

You may wonder to yourself what this has to do with cheerfulness. My answer is that the Bible speaks directly to this issue in Proverbs 17:22, "A cheerful heart is good medicine, but a crushed spirit dries up the bones." You are probably more familiar with the King James rendering of the first part of that verse: "A merry heart doeth good like medicine." Unfortunately, that rendering has become so familiar it has become a slogan without any meaning. We cross-stitch it and then put it on our walls, but we forget to ponder its message.

A look at the original Hebrew helps us dig out the message for today. When Solomon composed this verse, he used a verb form that could literally be translated, "A cheerful heart *causes good healing*."

Now that verse is three thousand years old. Isn't it amazing how Solomon, under the inspiration of the Holy Spirit, wrote something down that modern medical science is just discovering? *Twentieth-century research agrees with these ancient words of Solomon: There is a close relationship between the way you look at life and your own physical well-being.*

Consider also Proverbs 18:14: "A man's spirit sustains him in sickness, but a crushed spirit who can bear?" We all know people who struggle with sickness and weakness, yet when you go to see them, they cheer you up. They are down-and-out physically, but they actually make you feel better, for they are strong in spirit even though their bodies are wasting away. On the other hand, others are sick because their spirits are crushed. When you visit them, you feel worse when you leave than when you came, for they have sucked all the life out of you.

These verses are telling us that there is a basic relationship between your mental attitude and your physical well-being. Said another way, what you are in your heart has a direct bearing on your physical health. What is on the inside eventually manifests itself physically on the outside.

Solomon was nothing if not practical. A merry heart may help keep you out of the hospital. Think about that the next time you start feeling sick.

May the joy of the Lord be my strength so that I may have a merry heart no matter what happens today. Amen.

Do you have a merry heart? Would those who know you agree with your answer?

When you think of Proverbs 17:22, who comes to mind as a good example of the verse?

CHILDREN

---※---

Planting Seeds for God to Harvest

Train a child in the way he should go, and when he is old he will not turn from it.

Proverbs 22:6

What exactly do these famous words mean? I believe the key lies in the phrase *the way.* When Solomon uses those words he almost always means either "the way of righteousness" or "the way of wickedness." (For example, *see* 8:20; 10:29; 12:26; 14:12; 15:9.) To raise a child "in the way he should go" is to teach him to choose the path of righteousness and to reject the path of evil. We might state the meaning of the verse this way: *Children make many mistakes in the course of life, but those raised in a godly home will be inclined toward righteousness.* Christian parents need to take the long view when evaluating how their children are doing. Many teenagers and young adults go through a period of questioning values and testing limits. But the good seed planted in childhood will eventually bear fruit, though not necessarily as soon as we would like or as abundantly as we would like.

As you can tell, I am not among those who believe that children raised in a godly environment will automatically follow in the footsteps of their parents. But I firmly believe that we can "tip the scales" to our advantage so that our children have an inclination to follow the Lord when they are older.

Recently I was asked to find a biblical father who "did it right." That sounds simple, but it isn't, for the Bible doesn't tell us everything we'd like to know. For most of the men of the Bible, we'd have to say, "We don't know whether they were good fathers or not."

But if one criterion of good fatherhood is whether your son follows in your footsteps, then I would nominate Asa, king of Judah, as one father who did it right. To begin with, Asa did not grow up in a godly home. His father was a man named Abijah, about whom the Bible says, "He committed all the sins his father had done before him" (1 Kings 15:3). But that takes us back to Rehoboam, who introduced idolatry into Judah. And that takes us back to Solomon, a wise man with a divided heart.

So when Asa came onto the scene, he entered as the third generation after his great-grandfather. His father and grandfather had brought evil into the land. What would Asa do? The Bible says that he "did what was right in the eyes of the Lord, as his father David had done" (1 Kings 15:11). That takes us back four generations, to his great-great-grandfather.

What legacy did Asa leave behind? A son named Jehoshaphat. Which way would he go? Second Chronicles 20:32 tells us that "he walked in the ways of his father Asa and did not stray from them." I cannot imagine a better compliment.

Perhaps you are the first Christian in your family or

the first one in several generations. Are you worried about whether your children will follow you? The best thing parents can do for their sons or daughters is to give them an example worth following. By God's grace, the pattern of sin can be broken and a godly heritage established. Asa did, and so can you.

Lord God, help me to live so that those who come after me will know that I have followed You. Amen.

What kind of example did your parents leave for you? What are you doing to proactively train your children to choose the right path? If your closest friends followed your example, would they end up following the Lord?

COMPLAINING

✦

Don't Blame God for Your Problems

A man's own folly ruins his life, yet his heart rages against the Lord.

Proverbs 19:3

Here is a common problem. When things go bad for us, we start to blame God as if He were the source of all our problems. Like Adam in the Garden of Eden, we say, "It was the woman you gave me," forgetting all along that no one made us eat the fruit.

Complaining is counterproductive in many ways. First, it may turn us against God and block the flow of His blessing into our lives. Second, it may cause us to blame others instead of looking within for the source of our problems. Third, it may cause us to miss the lessons God is trying to teach us through the difficulties we encounter.

Hard times provide some of the most important lessons of spiritual growth. Several years ago a friend shared a statement that revolutionized my thinking in this area. It is deceptively simple: "When hard times come, be a student, not a victim." The more I ponder those words, the more profound they seem. Many people go through life as professional victims, always talking about how unfair life is.

A *victim* says, "Why did this happen to me?" A *stu-*

dent says, "What can I learn from this?"

A *victim* blames others for his problems. A *student* asks, "How much of this did I bring on myself?"

A *victim* looks at everyone else and cries out, "Life isn't fair." A *student* looks at life and says, "What happened to me could have happened to anybody."

A *victim* believes hard times have come because God is trying to punish him. A *student* understands that God allows hard times in order to help him grow.

A *victim* would rather complain than find a solution. A *student* has no time to complain because he is busy making the best of his situation.

A *victim* believes the deck of life is forever stacked against him. A *student* believes that God is able to reshuffle the deck anytime He wants to.

A *victim* feels so sorry for himself that he has no time for others. A *student* focuses on helping others so that he has no time to feel sorry for himself.

A *victim* begs God to remove all the problems of life so that he might be happy. A *student* has learned through the problems of life that God alone is the source of all true happiness.

Victims worry about what other people think of them. *Students* know that the only thing that matters is what God thinks of them.

Victims limp through life, complaining about their heavy burdens. *Students* race toward the finish line, looking to their reward.

Many things happen to us beyond our control. In

that sense, we are all victims of unexpected circumstances. Unfortunately, some people never rise above the victim mode. *But it doesn't have to be that way.* We have the opportunity to choose the way we respond to the things that happen to us. By the grace of God, we can decide to become students, not victims, as we face the trials of life.

O Lord, help me to be a student and not a victim today. Amen.

Are you a complainer? What would your friends say?

In what areas of life are you most tempted to be a victim? What can you do to become a student instead?

CONFESSION

---※---

Telling the Truth About Yourself

He who conceals his sins does not prosper, but whoever confesses and renounces them finds mercy.

Proverbs 28:13

The last words of each clause contain the most important truth. If you conceal your sin, you will not prosper. If you confess it and forsake it, you will find mercy. How hard it is to believe these words and to take them at face value. When we sin, everything within us screams out, "Cover it up. Turn off the lights. Bury the evidence. Destroy the tapes. Make up an alibi. Leave the scene of the crime. Run! Run! Run!"

Something in our spiritual bloodstream causes us to run from the pain of confession. When God confronted Adam with his sin, the first man made the first excuse in history: "The woman you put here with me—she gave me some fruit from the tree, and I ate it" (Genesis 3:12). Not a very noble answer. In the end he grudgingly confesses, but not before blaming Eve and, by implication, God.

Two key words deserve special attention. The first is *confess,* which means "to tell the whole truth." When we confess, we are not only admitting our sin; we are also agreeing with God's assessment of what we did. True confession begins with the notion that God is God and that we have knowingly violated His standards. The second word is *renounce,* which means "to abandon, forsake, desert, turn away from." True confession always leads to renunciation. If after confessing our sin we quickly return to it, or if we long to return to it, then we have missed the teaching of this verse and we will not find God's mercy.

Several years ago one of my brothers sent me some material from a Christian counselor. On one of the sheets he had done a takeoff on the words of Jesus in John 8:32, "You will know the truth, and the truth will set you free." The counselor had added the phrase: "The truth shall make you free . . . but it will hurt you first."

That strikes me as an extremely important insight. This explains why so many people struggle with their problems for years. They don't want the truth to hurt them . . . so they avoid the truth at all costs.

Do they want to get better? Absolutely.

Do they know the truth? Intellectually, yes.

Then why don't they get better? Because they won't let the truth get close enough to hurt them. Instead, they erect a thousand defense mechanisms that deflect the truth before it hits home.

Which explains why you can go to church for years, listen to sermons for years, read the Bible and pray for years—and still not get better. "The truth will set you free, but it will hurt you first." When you are finally willing to be hurt by the truth about yourself, then—and only then—will you be set free.

Most people don't enjoy confessing their sins, so they avoid it whenever possible. But when we dare to take God at His word, we discover the joy of forgiveness. If you are willing to tell the truth about yourself, you can be set free.

Heavenly Father, give me the grace to tell the truth so that Your grace might make me clean. Amen.

Is it getting easier for you to say, "I was wrong"?

Why is confession such a crucial part of the spiritual life? What happens when we refuse to confess our sins? What sin do you need to confess right now?

CONFIDENTIALITY

——————✦——————

How to Say Nothing Nicely

A gossip betrays a confidence, but a trustworthy man keeps a secret.

Proverbs 11:13

How good are you at keeping a secret? I don't mean a big, world-shaking secret, but the kind of secret you hear almost every day. Perhaps your best friend confides in you that he is thinking of changing jobs. Or your friend says that she and her husband are having marital problems. Or your boss confides in you that the company is about to relocate to another state. What do you do with that kind of information?

Let's face it—everyone loves a secret. We love to hear them and, unfortunately, we love to tell them. When someone says, "Let me tell you a secret," the world stops to listen.

Turn it around. What do you do when someone says, "I'm sorry. I promised I wouldn't tell." Be honest. It drives most of us up the wall, doesn't it? We can't stand to be left out. So we badger the person; we keep asking questions ("Don't tell me the whole thing, just tell me part of it"); we hound them until finally they give in.

We all know people who can't keep a secret. Some people love to share their tidbits of inside information to one person at a time. Others won't tell the whole secret, but will drop hints so you can figure it out on your own. Occasionally Christians reveal secrets by calling them prayer requests.

Here's a simple rule: If you promise to keep a secret, then keep it. If you don't intend to keep the secret, don't make the promise. If someone objects that a person must sometimes tell a secret for the good of everyone involved, the answer is yes, sometimes that happens, but not as often as we think.

The ability to keep a secret is a mark of maturity; the compulsion to reveal a secret is a mark of immaturity. And it also is a mark of maturity to respect a person who says, "I'm sorry. I can't tell you."

How about you? What is the level of your maturity? Are you the kind of person who can be trusted *not* to reveal confidential information? When a friend comes to you confessing serious personal problems, do you phone someone else so they can "pray about it?" Or are you strong enough to keep it to yourself?

These are searching questions. One reason hurting Christians often drift away from the church is that they simply cannot trust fellow believers to keep their struggles private. How many churches have split because someone began spreading rumors and revealing secrets! How many believers are defiled because we are too curious, too quick to pry, and too prone to repeat things in public that would be better dealt with in private.

God bless those believers who can keep a secret. They

bear a heavy burden that only God knows.

During World War II it was said that "loose lips sink ships." They also destroy lives, break up marriages, split churches, and ruin reputations.

Remember, you don't have to tell everything you know. If you can't keep a secret, don't listen to it in the first place.

Lord Jesus, I pray to become the kind of person others can trust with their secrets. Amen.

Do you find it hard to keep a secret? How do you feel when others refuse to tell the secrets they know?

In what sense do those who keep a secret bear a heavy burden?

What happens when people tell their secrets indiscriminately?

CONSCIENCE

❖

It Can Be the Voice of God

The lamp of the Lord searches the spirit of a man; it searches out his inmost being.

Proverbs 20:27

What is meant by "the lamp of the Lord"? There are two answers. First, it refers to human conscience, which "searches out" a man's motive, helping discern between good and evil. God has placed the light of conscience inside every heart. Romans 2:15 explains that the conscience, informed by the innate laws of God, sometimes accuses a person and sometimes excuses him. That means God has written on the heart of every man a basic moral code. That code is similar to the things contained in the Ten Commandments. This universal moral code consists of things like "Do not steal," "Do not cheat," "Tell the truth," "Honor your parents," "Keep your word," "Help the poor," "Do not kill," and so on. It would be hard to find a culture anywhere in the world where those moral values are not honored. God gives us a conscience so that we will live up to the moral values common to all mankind.

There is an ancient tale about a court magician who wanted to give his king a very special gift. After much work, he designed a magic ring which had a very special property. Every time the king had an evil thought or an unworthy ambition, the ring began to shrink tightly around his finger, thus warning him of impending danger.

The human conscience is like that. It is a ring around the heart that tightens every time we begin to violate our own standards. It warns of impending danger. We disregard our conscience at our own peril.

From the New Testament perspective, the "lamp of the Lord" also refers to the Holy Spirit, who, like a bright lamp, goes from one "room" of the heart to another, searching out those things that even conscience cannot discover. After all, a man may have a "seared conscience" and be a moral sociopath, totally unable to know right from wrong. Conscience is a good guide, but it is not infallible. The Holy Spirit sees and knows every thought and intent of the heart (*see* Hebrews 4:13). Nothing is hidden from Him. Like a blazing light, the Spirit of God exposes everything, sees everything, and drags the deepest secrets out of the closet and exposes them to the light of God. Proverbs 5:21 speaks of the same truth: "For a man's ways are in full view of the Lord, and he examines all his paths." To that we might add Proverbs 15:3: "The eyes of the Lord are everywhere, keeping watch on the wicked and the good."

This truth is both comforting and terrifying. To those who have nothing to hide, the lamp of the Lord holds no fear; but to those who have many "hidden things," the lamp of the Lord brings them all to the light sooner or later.

How should we then live? First, we should pay attention to our conscience, for it can keep us out of trouble. Second, since the Holy Spirit constantly searches our inmost being, let us live openly and honestly, hiding nothing. Then we will have nothing to fear.

Holy Spirit, search me, cleanse me, move within me until nothing is hidden and all things are laid bare before You. Amen.

How is the human conscience "the voice of God" to the soul? How does a conscience become "seared"?

Under what circumstances should we disregard our own conscience?

How can you become more responsive to the work of the Holy Spirit in your own life?

CONTENTMENT

---⟡---

Learning to Love Lima Beans

Better a dry crust with peace and quiet than a house full of feasting, with strife.

Proverbs 17:1

Better a meal of vegetables where there is love than a fattened calf with hatred.

Proverbs 15:17

Many people are confused about contentment, thinking that it means having what you want. Nothing could be further from the truth. Contentment is not having what you want, but wanting what you already have. Far too many of us measure our happiness by how things are going on the outside. The Bible says it is not like that. Contentment is a matter of understanding how much you already have.

These two verses teach us that it is better to eat cold lima beans where people love you than to have a T-bone steak where they can't stand to look at your face. This is why people get depressed at Thanksgiving and Christmastime, is why they hate to go back home. When they go back home, all the old hurts and bad feelings start coming out. What ought to be a joyful, happy time becomes an unbearable struggle.

What is contentment? Contentment is realizing that

you are better off the way you are right now. If you are dreaming of more money and bigger material possessions, contentment is realizing how much God has blessed you and how much you have right now.

One man journeyed with a cough that wouldn't go away and unusual weariness, so he went to the doctor for a checkup. Cancer. The diagnosis was ominous—something about a large-cell tumor on the thymus. Treatable, but not a moment to lose because this kind of cancer spreads rapidly.

First there was surgery to remove the tumor, followed by massive chemotherapy. How was it? Terrible. His hair fell out, he lost weight, he felt sicker than he had ever felt in his life, and at the end the nurses cheerily told him, "You're doing just great. Most people get really sick." The man replied that if there were something worse called "really sick," he didn't care to experience it. Finally, there was radiation where the tumor had been—a final attack to destroy any stray cancer cells.

Six years have passed and the cancer has not returned. His wife offered this comment on their ordeal: "When something like this happens, it puts all of life in a new perspective. You learn to live one day at a time. You start to enjoy the things you used to take for granted.

"As hard as this has been, we feel grateful that it happened. I never thought I'd say that, but it's true. Fighting cancer brought our family together and made us appreciate what we have. God has been so good to us," she said.

It is a timely lesson for all of us. Even the bad times

can be an occasion to experience the goodness of God, especially if we learn to appreciate what we already have.

> *Lord Jesus, do what is necessary so that we will learn to be happy with what we have, instead of dreaming of what we don't have. Amen.*

How happy are you right now? What would need to change in order for you to be happy?

Why is it that we often don't learn contentment until we go through hard times?

CONVICTION

❈

Do Right Though the Stars Fall

Fear of man will prove to be a snare, but whoever trusts in the Lord is kept safe.

Proverbs 29:25

The dictionary defines *conviction* as "a fixed or strong belief." It is the moral certainty that some things are right and others are wrong. A *conviction* is not the same thing as a *preference*, which is a personal opinion about the way things ought to be. Preferences often change; convictions rarely do.

Almost every day we are faced with a question such as this: Shall I do what I know to be right, in order to please God? Or will I neglect my convictions and do what I believe to be wrong, in order to please men? One hundred years ago William Arnot pointed out that while the knowledge of the truth is almost universal, the practice of what is right is rare. "Few act the answer which all agree to speak." If anything has changed in the last century, it is that we can no longer say that knowledge of the truth is almost universal; today it seems to be almost nonexistent.

In our day, we Christians are urged to tone down our language for fear that we might offend someone. Indeed, sometimes the followers of Christ appear to be so agreeable that we have completely lost the offense of the Cross.

In truth, I do not believe our problem today is that we are too offensive. With few exceptions, our problem lies almost entirely in the opposite direction. We aren't offensive enough. Or we aren't offensive about the right things.

What exactly is meant by the phrase *the fear of man?* Since most of our rewards in this life come from others, it is natural that we should want to please them. That tendency, while noble in some areas—such as doing good work, keeping our promises, and acting with compassion—is deadly in the spiritual realm. We may begin to think that discretion is the better part of valor in discussing eternal truth, and so may pass up opportunities to speak a word for the Savior. I heard recently about a top-level employee of a huge corporation who said that if you want to rise to the top, it would be better not to be outspoken about your Christian faith. Be discreet, don't say much, don't rock the boat; and when you get to the top—if you ever make it—then you can speak out.

But is that not what the fear of man is all about? When you finally make it to the top, you've grown so accustomed to not rocking the boat that it's easier to keep your mouth closed and sail on toward retirement.

The fear of man is a snare because it keeps us quiet when we ought to speak up. It's also a snare because we end up valuing the approval of the world over God's approval. Worst of all, it tricks us into thinking that this world is more important than the world to come.

Against all that are the simple words at the end of the verse: "Whoever trusts in the Lord is kept safe." God

Himself will take up your cause if you are not ashamed to take up His. You may not make it to the top, but you'll enjoy the journey much more because you'll know the Lord is on your side.

> *Lord Jesus, give us Your perfect balance of truth and love so that we may stand for the truth without embarrassment. Amen.*

Name a time when the fear of man kept you from being bold for the truth. What would you do differently next time?

Who is the most courageous person you know? Would anyone give your name as the answer to that question?

COOPERATION

❖

Working with Others on a Common Goal

Go to the ant, you sluggard; consider its ways and be wise!
Proverbs 6:6

L et's start with a piece of Bible trivia. How many times are ants mentioned the Bible? Ants are mentioned in only one book—once in Proverbs 6:6–8 and once in Proverbs 30:25.

Both references are worth considering. In Proverbs 6, Solomon invites us to study the ant for the purpose of learning wisdom. For instance, ants have no commanders (v. 7), yet they work together to store food for the winter (v. 8). Proverbs 30:25 makes a similar point: "Ants are creatures of little strength, yet they store up their food in the summer." How do the ants with little strength manage to store enough food to make it through the long winter months? The answer is, they start early, they look to the future, they pool their strength, and they work together for the common good.

Several years ago I had a chance to see this for myself. As I was taking an afternoon walk, I looked down and saw a vast army of ants carrying an earthworm. It was so startling that I stopped to watch the action.

The earthworm—shaped more or less like a treble clef—appeared to have dried out in the sun. All around the earthworm were ants, pushing away. And they were moving it one micro-inch at a time. I didn't count, but I would bet there were at least fifty ants pushing away at that poor dead earthworm. All around them were other ants, several hundred of them, "junior varsity" ants waiting for their chance to get in the game.

As I watched, they slowly pushed that worm toward the grassy edge of the sidewalk. I didn't stay for the denouement, but I suppose the ants feasted on filet of earthworm that night. There was certainly enough food to feed the whole colony for many days to come.

One thought lingered in my mind: A single ant is no match for an earthworm. As Proverbs 30:25 says, "Ants are creatures of little strength." A single ant could push for a year and never move an earthworm off the sidewalk. But what one ant couldn't do, many ants did by working together. Which is why Proverbs 6:6 says, "Go to the ant, you sluggard; consider its ways and be wise!"

By the way, it's no accident that I saw the ants during the summer. You can't find many earthworms in Chicago in January. The ants know that (with an instinct placed in them by God), so they gather their food early in preparation for the cold weather that must eventually come. Solomon saw the same thing I did, and he praised the ants because "they store up their food in the summer."

There's a lesson here about individual weakness and united strength. There's also a lesson about the value of working together to accomplish the greater good. And finally, there's also a lesson about preparing for the future.

An old children's song says, "The ants go marching two by two, hurrah, hurrah." Indeed they do, which is why they teach us that we can accomplish so much more when we work together.

As You have placed me in the body of Christ, Lord, so teach me to depend upon my brothers and sisters to accomplish Your work. Amen.

Name a time recently when, by working with others, you accomplished a significant task.

Would your friends say that you are better at cooperation or competition?

COSIGNING

❖

A Really Bad Idea

Do not be a man who strikes hands in pledge or puts up security for debts; if you lack the means to pay, your very bed will be snatched from under you.

Proverbs 22:26–27

Casual readers are often surprised to discover how much the book of Proverbs has to say about the dangers of cosigning. What might seem to us a relatively minor issue obviously didn't seem that way to Solomon. In order to help us get the big picture, here are some of the main verses on this topic:

> My son, if you have put up security for you neighbor, if you have struck hands in pledge for another, . . . go and humble yourself; . . . Free yourself, like a gazelle from the hand of the hunter. (6:1–5)

> He who puts up security for another will surely suffer, but whoever refuses to strike hands in pledge is safe. (11:15)

> A man lacking in judgment strikes hands in pledge and puts up security for his neighbor. (17:18)

Take the garment of one who puts up security for a stranger; hold it in pledge if he does it for a wayward woman. (20:16)

Why so many warnings? (1) Cosigning is easy to do. (2) It causes you to be financially dependent upon the actions of another person. (3) You may be taken in by an unscrupulous con artist. (4) It could actually encourage unfaithfulness on the part of the other person because he knows you are there to pay the debt if he defaults. (5) It can lead to public humiliation and personal bankruptcy.

These verses are not meant to ban generous giving to a friend in need. Far from it. But cosigning (or "striking the hands" in a promise) is more like gambling than giving. In many cases, a man may cosign a note, hoping to see some exorbitant return on his investment. Or he may do it because he wants to help his friend out of a difficult situation.

But the warning could not be clearer. Cosigning exposes you to unusual risk with no real return. If you pledge your fortune on behalf of a "neighbor," you lack judgment; if you do it for a stranger, you deserve to lose your shirt; if you do it for a wayward woman, you may end up losing more than your sheets.

What about cosigning for a son or a daughter? Proverbs does not address that issue specifically. However, the general principle still applies. Giving is always better than cosigning. Many years ago I remember hearing a famous preacher tell of all the money he had loaned to young ministerial students, many of whom did not (or would not) repay him. He carried their IOUs around in his wallet, but every time he looked at those slips of paper, he felt a bit of anger at all the unpaid debts. Finally, one day he simply took all the slips of paper out of his wallet, tore them up, and threw them away. That simple act liberated him completely. No one owed him any money because the debts had been canceled. What had once been a loan was now a gift. If they chose to repay him, fine. If not, it didn't matter. From that day forward he never again loaned money to anyone. If he had it to give, he gave it. If not, he refused to loan it. Thus he was able to be generous and have a clear conscience at the same time.

Solomon would approve of that attitude. Cosigning isn't a sin, but it's foolish and almost always unnecessary. Far better to be generous when you can and let God take care of your financial needs.

Lord, I pray for the gift of generosity so that I can give to those who have genuine needs. Amen.

Do you agree with Solomon about the dangers of cosigning? Why or why not? Do you agree that generosity is wiser than cosigning?

Have you ever cosigned a loan (or asked someone to cosign for you)? How did your experience turn out?

COUNSEL

God's Gift to Fools

Plans fail for lack of counsel, but with many advisers they succeed.

Proverbs 15:22

This particular piece of advice is repeated several times in Proverbs. The wise man listens to advice from others (12:15), accepts instruction (19:20), and proactively seeks out wise counsel before embarking on a major project (20:18) because he understands that no plan can succeed without the Lord's blessing (21:30). Finally, he takes great joy in listening to the advice of his friends (27:9).

I have a few friends in my life who are like that. Every time they speak, they speak wisdom and knowledge. Some of them are people I have known for twenty or thirty years. Some of them are people I don't talk to very often. Some of them are people I may not talk to except once every ten years. But because they are people of wisdom and knowledge, I know that if I have not talked to them for ten years, I can go back to them and say, "What do you think about this?" Because their lips speak wisdom and knowledge, they can say, "I don't think you should do this; I don't think you do that; have you thought about this?" Invariably, when I talk to people like that, my life is enriched because the lips of the righteous bring forth wisdom and knowledge. Blessed are you if you have a few people in your life who can speak wisdom and knowledge to you. You are doubly blessed if you have the ability to speak wisdom and knowledge to other people.

What is the difference between a wise man and a fool? The fool thinks he knows it all; the wise man knows he doesn't. The fool refuses instruction because he's got his whole plan laid out in his mind and he doesn't want to be bothered with anyone else's opinion. The wise man knows that his plans aren't perfect, so he isn't embarrassed to ask for advice.

Seeking counsel has many benefits. It gives us another set of eyes and ears; it buys us time to think of alternatives. We may uncover an entirely new perspective or possibly a new set of facts to consider. Certainly wise counselors will produce in us a new sense of humility.

After we have received wise counsel, evaluated our plans, and adjusted them accordingly, we may move forward with new confidence because our plans have been tested even before we put them in place.

No one knows everything. No one has all the knowledge. But God gave each of us a little piece of the big picture. The more pieces we put together in advance, the greater our chances for success.

So before you make a big decision, pick up the phone and call a few friends. Ask for help. Let them take a free shot at your new idea. If it's a good one, it will stand the test. If it's not, you can change it or forget about it. Either way, you come out ahead.

Father, thank You for friends who care enough to give wise advice. Please give me an open heart to graciously receive what they say. Amen.

Who gives you counsel when you face a big decision? Who comes to you for counsel?

What principles do you use to sift out the good from the bad? Have you ever ignored the advice of your friends on a major issue? What happened?

COURAGE

✦

How to Face Down Your Fears

The wicked man flees though no one pursues, but the righteous are as bold as a lion.

Proverbs 28:1

The dictionary defines courage this way: The ability to face and deal with a dangerous or difficult situation. There are two parts. First you must face difficulty; then you must deal with it.

Most of the popular images of courage have to do with men fighting on a battlefield. The soldiers coming ashore at Omaha Beach. The defenders of Bastogne holding out against the Nazis. The Marines landing on Iwo Jima. Pickett's charge at Gettysburg. President Kennedy standing strong during the Cuban Missile Crisis.

I have thought much about the many faces of courage—most of them ones you never see on a battlefield. Courage is a family dealing with terminal cancer. It is a single mother struggling to raise her family. It is a widow who faces the last years of her life without her beloved husband by her side. It is a child of divorce, struggling with his self-image, with doubt and anger, and with feelings of rejection. It is a single person who chooses purity over promiscuity. It is an engaged couple who will wait even though the world says go ahead. It is former President Reagan telling the nation that he had been diagnosed with Alzheimer's disease. It is a newly-minted MBA who moves into an inner-city community. It is an employee who sees corruption and has the courage to blow the whistle. It is a dad facing a difficult surgery.

What do these things have in common? I see four qualities that are evident in people with courage:

1. Bravery in the face of danger: "I won't be afraid."
2. Steadfastness in the face of opposition: "I won't give up."
3. Action in the face of resistance: "I won't be intimidated."
4. Optimism in the face of despair: "I won't lose heart."

Where does this courage come from? Proverbs 28:1 tells us that "the righteous are as bold as a lion." The righteous are bold, not the wicked. The wicked are scared to death. If you are a Christian, the first step to courage is to remember who you are in Jesus Christ. You are victorious, accepted, justified, redeemed, saved, and completely forgiven. Your sins are washed away. You are seated with Jesus Christ in the heavenlies. You were born for courage, not for fear. Second Timothy 1:7 tells us that God has not given us a spirit of fear, but of power, love, and self-discipline. If you have a controlling spirit of fear, timidity, or anxiety, it didn't come from God, for He does not give His people a spirit of fear.

There is an old Italian proverb that goes this way:

Better to spend one day as a lion than one hundred years as a sheep. Better to spend one day with courageous faith in God than a whole lifetime cowering in fear.

You will never win until you rise up and confront the thing that is dragging you down. God put courage in you the moment you came to Christ. Use the courage God has given you, and you will be able to face your fears and come out victorious.

Holy Spirit, I ask that You fill me with love, power, and self-discipline, so that I can face the future without fear. Amen.

Name the three greatest fears in your life.

How would your life be different if you began to face your fears?

COURTESY

❖

The Milk of Human Kindness

If a man loudly blesses his neighbor early in the morning, it will be taken as a curse.

Proverbs 27:14

There is a bit of mystery surrounding this particular proverb. Is the man in view simply a gregarious friend who is just a little too happy early in the morning? Or is there a sinister implication here, that this man is being falsely friendly in order to gain a personal advantage? Is he too friendly too early because he wants to take you off guard while you are still waking up? The *New Living Translation* evidently inclines to the first view, translating the verse this way: "If you shout a pleasant greeting to your neighbor too early in the morning, it will be counted as a curse!"

So what's the problem? At the very least, your gregarious neighbor is showing a deplorable lack of common courtesy. Even if he means well, his timing is off by about two hours. Harry Ironside calls this behavior "utterly obnoxious." Such a person is tone-deaf to the delicate sensitivities of friendship. There is a proper time for everything—including hearty greetings—but this man evidently doesn't know or doesn't care.

Proverbs contains several other examples of this

boorish behavior. Overfamiliarity can be a problem (25:17), as can an overused sense of humor (26:18–19). Sometimes the problem is simply making inappropriate comments (25:20). All of us may be guilty of such things occasionally. Wisdom senses the problems before they arise and finds a graceful alternative.

John Henry Newman commented that "it is almost a definition of a gentleman to say that he is one who never inflicts pain." Because he possesses a keen understanding of human nature, he knows when to speak, when to be silent, when to drop in for a visit, and when to go home. He doesn't wear out his welcome, and he doesn't use humor as a tool to hurt others. To use an old expression, he "wears well."

First Corinthians 13:4–5 tells us that "love is kind" and "is not rude." Courtesy is nothing more than the practical application of Christian love to the ordinary affairs of life. The dictionary calls courtesy "excellence of manners" and "polite behavior." It is a combination of tact, timing, sensitivity, and kindness. Courteous people are known not only by what they do and say, but also by what they don't do and don't say.

Admittedly, this virtue may not seem as noble as courage or as important as integrity. But when analyzed, courtesy is impossible without a whole host of other virtues, including patience, forgiveness, self-control, and humility. When someone spreads rumors about you, are you strong enough not to retaliate in anger? If a gregarious neighbor knocks at your door at 6:15 A.M., will you be gracious enough not to pour hot coffee down his pants?

In a very real sense, the test of courtesy is the bad manners of others. Anyone can be courteous to nice people. It's how you respond to the cads and louts of the world that makes all the difference.

"Life is short," said Ralph Waldo Emerson, "but there is always time for courtesy." That's a good thing to remember the next time your neighbor knocks at your door.

Lord Jesus, You were the epitome of courtesy toward friend and foe alike. Give me the grace to treat others as You would. Amen.

List four or five examples of common courtesy and rate yourself in each area.

How do you normally respond to discourteous treatment by others?

DEPENDABILITY

❖

How Old Faithful Got Its Name

He who tends a fig tree will eat its fruit, and he who looks after his master will be honored.

Proverbs 27:18

It has been well said that the greatest ability is dependability. The word itself means "able to be relied upon." It's the one quality every boss prizes in his workers. Talent counts and education matters, but they don't mean as much as dependability. Find a man who can take a job and carry it through to the end. Mark that man, note his name, jot it down so you won't forget it. Sooner or later he will rise to the top. He will "eat the fruit" of his own labor. Second Timothy 2:6 says it very plainly: "The hardworking farmer should be the first to receive a share of the crops." Dependability always brings its own reward. If you can do the job and do it well and do it without having to be reminded or cajoled or promised or bribed or threatened; if you simply show up day after day and do your job, you will eventually "eat the fruit" of your labor.

So many of us make excuses for nonperformance. We were too busy; we didn't understand; it didn't seem very important; we had other things to do; our desk was so cluttered that we lost the file; we never learned that particular computer program; we weren't feeling well, so we decided to go home early; we had a better idea; the guys in top management are goldbricks; the boss doesn't appreciate us, so why put ourselves out for him? On and on we go, making excuses for what we didn't do.

Meanwhile, the man next to us steadily goes about his work. He's not flashy or especially clever; in fact, we could probably work circles around him if we tried. But while we're frittering away the day, he's sitting at his desk, working on the phone, writing the report, fixing the machine, seeing the patients, calling his contacts, preparing his lesson plans. He doesn't overpromise and underdeliver. If he says he can do it, you can take it to the bank.

Like Old Faithful, he simply shows up on time and does his job. Guess who gets the promotion? Or the bonus at the end of the year? Guess whose job is safe when downsizing hits your department?

It's not you. You've been too busy finding reasons not to do your job. Meanwhile, he's been plugging away day after day.

God bless that man and give him his due. Because he tended the fig tree, he gets to enjoy the harvest. His master is pleased and gives him a raise.

There's nothing magical about this. He was dependable and was rewarded. That ought to be your story. If it's not, you've got some explaining to do.

Father, You always keep Your promises. Help me to keep mine. Amen.

Bottom line: Are you a dependable person? What would your spouse say? Your friends? Your boss? Your fellow employees? If you don't know the answer, ask them.

What steps do you need to take to become more dependable?

DILIGENCE

❖

Staying by the Stuff

Lazy hands make a man poor, but diligent hands bring wealth.

Proverbs 10:4

Ponder this definition of diligence: "Long, steady application to one's occupation or studies; persistent effort." That's clear, isn't it? If you want to make it to the top in any field of endeavor, you need many things working in your favor. Some of them can't be orchestrated but must be supplied by the Lord's providential favor. However, Solomon teaches us that you can tip the scales of life in your favor through "long, steady application" and "persistent effort."

Often that will require persistence in the face of doubt and ridicule. Michelangelo took a piece of marble that no one else could use and eventually produced the incomparable *David*. Christopher Columbus ignored his critics and eventually discovered America. Skeptics tried to convince Henry Ford to abandon his idea of a mass-produced motorcar. People laughed at Wilbur and Orville Wright when they attempted to create a flying machine. But in each case diligence won the day.

Most of us have heard the story of Thomas Edison and the invention of the incandescent light bulb. For months he struggled to find the proper material for the filament inside the bulb. Nothing seemed to work. Some materials would conduct electricity but wouldn't produce light; others produced light but immediately burned up. Month after month he stayed in his laboratory in Menlo Park, New Jersey, doggedly trying one combination after another. Eventually he had tried 799 different combinations. "Don't you feel like you've wasted your time?" someone asked him. "Oh no," Edison replied, "now I know 799 things that won't work."

In a recent article in *Leaders for Today,* Harold Keown examined the lives of Christian leaders from many countries and asked how it was that, in the face of intense opposition, they accomplished so much for Jesus Christ. His conclusion startled me: "People serious about achieving seemingly impossible goals often assume the stance of a turtle."

It sounds strange because turtles seem like anything but a role model for outstanding achievers. But it's true. As Aesop pointed out several thousand years ago, the turtle plods along even though he is soon passed by the swift-running hare. But who gets to the finish line first? The turtle, because he just kept on going. That's a turtle truism: Successful people just keep on going despite the opposition, despite their apparent lack of progress, despite the fact that others pass them by. They stay the course, keep moving ahead, always marching toward godly goals.

Calvin Coolidge summed it up well when he said,

"Nothing in the world can take the place of persistence. Talent will not; nothing is more common than unsuccessful men with talent. Genius will not; unrewarded genius is almost a proverb. Education will not; the world is full of educated derelicts. Persistence and determination alone are omnipotent."

Philippians 4:13 says, "I can do all things through Christ which strengtheneth me" (KJV). Do you feel defeated today, trapped on a dead-end street? Remember the turtle and take hope. You can do more than you think you can.

> Lord God, forgive me for giving up too soon. Create in me new determination to keep on moving in the right direction. Amen.

Have you ever known someone who succeeded in some worthwhile project through nothing more than sheer determination and persistence?

Can you think of a part of your life where you are currently tempted to give up too soon? What do you need to do about it?

DISCERNMENT

❖

When You're in a Hole, Stop Digging

A discerning man keeps wisdom in view, but a fool's eyes wander to the ends of the earth.

Proverbs 17:24

The particular Hebrew word translated "discerning" in this verse is very common in the Old Testament. It has the idea of considering a situation carefully, studying all the options, pondering possible courses of action, and then choosing the best course. By contrast, a fool pays no attention to anything around him but blithely lets his mind wander, and so stumbles from one predicament to another.

A father was talking with his son about sound financial principles when the question arose: What do you do when you are already in debt? The answer is not hard to find: Get out of debt as quickly as possible. The father coined a pithy aphorism he called the First Rule of Holes: "When you're in a hole, stop digging."

It makes sense, doesn't it? When you find yourself in a financial hole, stop digging! You're already in a hole. Don't make matters worse by using your credit cards. If you want to get out of the hole, your first step is to make sure you're not digging yourself in deeper.

The same principle applies across the board. What's

the first step in losing weight? Stop digging! You're already in a hole and it's a tight fit because your waistline has expanded. Lay off the fat, forget about sweets for a while, and stock up on alfalfa sprouts.

Not long ago someone asked me a very pointed question. This person had been involved in a pattern of sinful behavior. In all seriousness, he wanted to know why he should stop, since he had been doing it for such a long time. My answer was simple: If I were talking to a thief, I would tell him to stop stealing. If I were speaking to a murderer, I would say, "Stop killing." If a student has been cheating on final exams, I would say, "Stop cheating." The first step in changing your behavior is to stop the destructive actions that have gotten you in the mess you are in.

When Jesus met the woman caught in adultery (John 8:1–11), He didn't condemn her, but He didn't condone her behavior, either. After routing her accusers He told her, "Neither do I condemn you. Go now and leave your life of sin" (v. 11). Was this woman forgiven by Jesus? I believe she was. Did she have a new life? Yes, she did. But in point of fact, she had suddenly come from immorality into a relationship with Jesus Christ. He would not condemn her, for she had condemned herself by her sin. But now that new life must be evidenced by a radical change in behavior: "Go and sin no more."

Are you suffering from anger and bitterness? Do you feel trapped by repeated failure? Would you like to see true change in your life? Are you in trouble—morally, spiritually, financially, emotionally, or relationally? There are many things that you can do to help yourself. But none of them will do any good until you remember the First Rule of Holes: When you're in a hole, stop digging.

Lord, I need Your help to stop doing the things that are hurting me so that I can begin to do the things that will make me better. Amen.

What "holes" are in you right now? Have you stopped digging yet?

In what areas of your life do you need discernment?

DISCIPLINE

✿

Spare the Rod and Spoil the Child

He who spares the rod hates his son, but he who loves him is careful to discipline him.

Proverbs 13:24

Discipline your son, and he will give you peace; he will bring delight to your soul.

Proverbs 29:17

Proverbs contains several verses that speak to the issue of corporal punishment. "Folly is bound up in the heart of a child, but the rod of discipline will drive it far from him" (22:15). "Do not withhold discipline from a child; if you punish him with the rod, he will not die. Punish him with the rod and save his soul from death" (23:13–14). "The rod of correction imparts wisdom, but a child left to himself disgraces his mother" (29:15).

Several observations are in order. First, corporal punishment is a mark of parental love. And more particularly, a refusal to administer such punishment may actually demonstrate a shameful lack of concern. Second, corporal punishment wisely administered has eternal benefits. It saves a soul from death—doubtless physical death is mainly in view, but it also extends to the spiritual realm. Third, the "rod of discipline" stands for more than the act of spanking. It represents the entire process of leading a child to moral and spiritual maturity. Fourth, any discipline exercised in uncontrolled anger can only breed further rebellion (see Colossians 3:21). Fifth, corporal punishment by itself can do little good. It must be accompanied by a wise master plan of teaching God's truth to your children. Sixth, parents who fail to discipline their children may end up disgraced and dishonored.

Certainly some parents go too far in the area of physical discipline. Some children have been scarred for life (literally and figuratively) by angry parents who took their frustrations out on unsuspecting boys and girls. It's important to understand that nothing in the Bible supports any kind of physical abuse—no matter what reason is given.

Solomon offers a number of wise guidelines. Discipline must spring from love and must be carefully done. Discipline is administered with a rod, not with a bare hand. Corporal punishment is only one small part of training up a child (Proverbs 22:6)—but it is an important part.

My junior high PE teacher had a wooden paddle with a taped handle that could be administered to an offender's rear end with incredible accuracy. The memory is vivid precisely because one day he caught me and a friend fooling around with some shuffleboard equipment. He didn't get mad; he didn't yell; he didn't lose his temper. He simply said the two most dreaded words in the English language: "Bend over." It was a mark of manhood not to cry, but the tears came squeezing out of my eyes nonetheless. The punishment had its intended effect. From that day till this, I've never messed with shuffleboard equipment again.

Let's keep a biblical balance in this area. Corporal punishment is not only allowed but encouraged for disobedient children. But it must be done carefully and thoughtfully, not in anger but in complete self-control. Properly administered, a spanking can be just as loving as a kiss.

> *Lord, give me the wisdom to discipline my children in the right way at the right time for the right reasons. Amen.*

How did your parents discipline you when you were growing up? Do they offer a good model to follow?

What guidelines are appropriate in administering corporal punishment?

ENDURANCE

Hanging Tough in Hard Times

If you falter in times of trouble, how small is your strength!
Proverbs 24:10

I have a couple of friends who love to run marathons. I have listened with amazement as they described the months of rigorous training necessary just to survive the twenty-six-mile ordeal. You must run hundreds of miles in preparation, follow a special diet, forego many of life's normal pleasures, and focus like a laser beam on the appointed day when you will punish your body almost to the breaking point. If others laugh, if they do not understand, if they think you have lost your mind, well and good; let them think what they will. You have committed yourself to running the marathon, and nothing can stand in your way.

My friends tell me that many of those who start out to run a marathon never make it. Most falter and drop out somewhere in the months before the race begins. Others start the race but never finish. A few will come agonizingly close to the finish line and then fall exhausted on the track.

Times of trial reveal what is in us. *We grow faster in hard times than we do in good times.* Romans 5:3–5 describes the process God uses to develop godly character in our lives. In fact, Paul says that "we also rejoice in our suffering" (v. 3). That may appear to be a misprint, but it isn't. He isn't suggesting that we should become masochists who rejoice in the hard times as if we enjoyed the pain. That wouldn't even be a Christian idea. He doesn't say, "We also rejoice *because of* our sufferings," but rather, "We also rejoice *in* our sufferings." Even in the most difficult moments, God's people can rejoice because He is at work doing something important in us. The next few verses explain the process. Suffering produces perseverance, perseverance produces character, character produces hope, and, verse 5 says, "Hope does not disappoint us." Why is that, Paul? "Because God has poured out his love into our hearts by the Holy Spirit." What starts with suffering ends with the love of God. This is a wonderful progression, but you can't get to the love of God without starting in the place of suffering.

More than one person has said to me, "I wouldn't trade my pain for the things God has shown me." If that doesn't make sense to you, it's only because you haven't been there yet.

I can testify that the most beautiful Christians I know are not the young, the rich, the educated, the successful, or the influential. Those may be happy but their lives are shallow, for the sculptor has not yet picked up the hammer and the chisel.

The most beautiful Christians I know are those who have been through suffering and come through it with their faith in God intact. They may not laugh as much as others, and their faces may be lined with care, but the beauty of Christ is in their eyes, and their voices testify to God's amazing grace.

The main thing is not to collapse under the pressure. Don't stop short of the finish line. Better days are coming if you just keep running.

Lord of all grace, I look to You for the strength I need to keep on going, for without Your help I will certainly fall. Amen.

In what areas of your life are you tempted to stop running the race? What would help you press on to the finish line?

Who are the most beautiful Christians you know? What makes them so special in your eyes?

ENVY

✦

The Green-Eyed Monster

A heart at peace gives life to the body, but envy rots the bones.

Proverbs 14:30

Envy rots the bones. The Hebrew literally means "envy makes the bones disintegrate." Once again, Solomon is telling us that there is a strong connection between the spiritual and the physical. The attitude of the heart has a direct impact on your physical well-being or lack thereof. If your heart is at peace, it gives life to the body. Envy causes the bones of the body to disintegrate.

King Saul is Exhibit A of a man whose life was destroyed by envy. You'll remember the little ditty that made Saul so angry when he realized that David had become more popular than he. As the women welcomed their returning heroes, they sang, "Saul has slain his thousands, and David his tens of thousands" (1 Samuel 18:7). When Saul heard that, his anger burned within him. Jealousy drove him to attempt to murder David. *Envy ate away at his insides until it finally destroyed him and his whole family.*

If you read 1 Samuel 10–26, you will discover some amazing things about Saul.

- He was in many respects a gifted man.
- He was tall and handsome.
- He was a natural leader of men.
- He was skillful in battle.
- He was chosen by God to be the first king of Israel.

In many ways he had *all the natural attributes for success*—plus he had the power of the Holy Spirit in his life. Yet we remember him as a failure because of the way his life ended. There were many contributing factors, but in the end his anger destroyed his life. After it became clear that David would replace him as king, Saul's heart was so *blinded by rage* that he could think of only one thing—killing David. So he hunted David as he would a wild animal, chasing him into the Judean desert, tracking him to a cave by the Dead Sea, a place called En Gedi. There David cut off a corner of Saul's robe when he actually could have killed him. David meant it as a sign of mercy, but Saul continued to hunt him down. Even though Saul knew that David would be the next king, his hatred so consumed him that he tried to kill him anyway. In the end, Saul and his sons were killed by the Philistines on the slopes of Mount Gilboa. The Philistines cut off his head, put his armor in a pagan temple, and fastened his headless corpse to the wall of Beth Shan. *It was an ignominious end for a man with the seeds of greatness in him.* Saul had many flaws, but it was his envy that finally destroyed him.

There are people who suffer deeply, both physically

and spiritually, because they will not forgive. Envy rots the bones. Anger rots the bones. Unforgiveness rots the bones. Bitterness rots the bones. Until you do something about your anger and bitterness, you're going to be sick, for the Bible says it will happen that way—it will literally rot your bones.

The lesson is clear: Don't let this happen to you!

Lord God, when I am tempted to envy, remind me that the only thing that matters is what You think of me. Amen.

Have you ever known anyone like Saul, whose life was destroyed by envy and jealousy?

Whom do you envy, if only just a tiny bit? Why? What does that teach you about yourself?

EQUALITY

❋

We're All in This Together

Rich and poor have this in common: The Lord is the Maker of them all.

Proverbs 22:2

This same thought is expressed in a slightly different manner in 29:13, "The poor man and the oppressor have this in common: The Lord gives sight to the eyes of both." If you put the rich and poor together and study them from a distance, they appear to be quite different and to be moving in different directions. From the moment of birth the poor man struggles to survive in a hostile world. He fights for every scrap of bread and toils around the clock simply to afford the bare necessities of life. Meanwhile, the rich man enters the world with a silver spoon in his mouth. He wants for nothing. Indeed, he has only to wish and his wish comes true. He is surrounded by friends, admirers, courtiers, groupies, and wannabes. But the poor man? He has few friends and no one to take up his cause. Solomon commented on this undeniable fact of life: "The poor are shunned even by their neighbors, but the rich have many friends" (14:20).

Solomon wrote those words three thousand years ago, but they could well have been written last week. No one can deny that there is a huge gap between the rich and poor today. The rich have their own subdivisions, their own schools, their own exclusive clubs, their own stores, and their own entertainment. They don't mix with the poor, and the poor don't mix with them.

But to reason that way is to leave God out of the picture. When you look from the standpoint of eternity, the rich and poor are much more alike than different. They have the same Maker, who gives life equally. They come into the world in exactly the same way, and they leave in the same way. In the cradle and in the grave, rich and poor lie side by side.

They are made of the same dust, and to that dust they will one day return. They are both sinners standing in desperate need of a Savior. If it is true that they clothe themselves differently, underneath the clothing their hearts are one and the same. When hungry, they both must eat; when weary, they both must rest. The differences in this regard are only in quality and quantity—their basic needs are precisely the same.

When the day comes that the poor man must leave this world, he will stand before the same God as the rich man. In that moment, the rich man's riches will be of no advantage and the poor man's poverty will be no hindrance.

The lesson is obvious and should be repeated for the benefit of rich and poor alike. The outward things of this world—those individual markers of money, power, family background, reputation, ethnic background, race, color, and national origin—do not tell the true story of a man or woman. They are at best temporary indicators—nothing more. In Christ Jesus there is neither Jew nor Gentile, slave nor free, male nor female, rich nor poor, black nor white, nor any other color.

In heaven we will mingle in complete equality with the whole family of God. It only makes sense to get started now.

Lord Jesus, I pray for a heart as big as Yours to love others as You have loved me. Amen.

How do you define prejudice, and why should it be considered a sin? How have you encountered prejudice in your own experience?

What step could you take this week to reach out across racial, ethnic, or economic lines?

EVANGELISM

❖

He Who Wins Souls Is Wise

The fruit of the righteous is a tree of life, and he who wins souls is wise.

Proverbs 11:30

The phrase "tree of life" takes us back to the very beginning of the Bible. Genesis 2 tells us that God planted the "tree of life" in the center of the Garden of Eden. If Adam and Eve had eaten the fruit of that tree, they would have lived forever (Genesis 3:22). The "tree of life" appears again in Revelation 22 in the New Jerusalem, the dwelling place of God's people throughout eternity. So the Bible begins and ends with the "tree of life."

But in between, every believer is called to be a "tree of life." The expression refers to the life-giving influence we can have on those around us. In the same way that we are to be salt and light in the midst of decay and darkness (Matthew 5:13–16), we are also called to be life-givers to those who are spiritually dead.

This is the greatest privilege any Christian can ever have—to lead another person to Jesus Christ. To use the terminology of Proverbs 11:30, you have "won" his soul for the Lord; you can truly be called a "soul-winner."

After preaching a sermon on prayer, I received the following message from a member of my congregation:

I wanted to share with you something interesting that happened a few days ago. Last Saturday afternoon my wife and I happened to park our car near the church before we went downtown. While we were walking back to our car, we happened to be discussing your sermon from last Sunday on prayer. I didn't even notice a man sitting on the bench by the sidewalk. As we were getting into our car, the man said that he overheard us talking about prayer and that he could use some prayer right now. So we sat down and talked with him. We spent about 30 minutes with him. He told us that he was down on his luck and that he felt like he needed prayer. So we prayed with him. We asked him if he knew Jesus and he said no. So we explained God's salvation plan and he prayed with us and accepted Jesus into his heart. I thought you might like to know that it was discussing your sermon on prayer that caused him to ask us to pray with him. It's great how God can work.

This wonderful story offers many good lessons. It reinforces the truth that there are hungry hearts all around us. There is no shortage of lost people in the world. All God needs is someone willing to spread the Word.

Sometimes we make evangelism more difficult than it really is. Let the image of the "tree of life" be a guide. Put your roots down deep in the soil of God's Word. As the fruit of a new life begins to appear, it will attract others. When they start asking questions, tell them about

Jesus. If they are ready, lead them to Christ.

Solomon said, "He who wins souls is wise." This is why Jesus came—to seek and to save the lost. Will you join Him in this great work?

Lead me to some soul today. O teach me, Lord, just what to say. Make me a "tree of life," I pray. Amen.

Who were the "trees of life" God used to bring you to Jesus? Have you ever thanked them for their godly influence?

Who are three people you would like to see come to Christ? Stop right now and pray that God would make you a "tree of life" to them.

8/17/98

EXCELLENCE

❖

Doing Your Best All the Time

Do you see a man skilled in his work? He will serve before kings; he will not serve before obscure men.

Proverbs 22:29

Children and young adults need to memorize this verse because we are told over and over that it's not *what* you know, it's *who* you know. There is some truth to that. But a more fundamental truth is this: The key to success in life is finding out what it is that you like to do—your passion in life—and then becoming very good at it. Be skilled in what excites you, for once you have determined what God has gifted you to do, if you will do it well, you will not serve before obscure men. You will rise until you serve before kings.

Talent matters, and so does giftedness, and it certainly helps if you have friends who can open doors of opportunity for you. But woe to the man who thinks that is all he needs to get ahead in life. The people who rise to the top and stay there are those who pay the price in long hours of study, preparation, and practice. This principle is true in every occupation. The best doctors, the finest lawyers, the most respected business leaders, the skaters who win the gold medals, the managers who consistently push their departments to meet their quotas, the teachers whose classes are filled every semester—these all share a commitment to excellence that begins with hard work and dedication.

Luck is what happens when preparation meets opportunity. I find it encouraging that excellence doesn't depend on anyone else but me. Every day when I get up I have a new opportunity to perform with excellence. If I don't, I can't blame anyone else.

In this verse God promises us that skillful work will not go unrewarded. First Samuel 16:14–23 records the story of David playing the harp to soothe Saul's tormented soul. David was chosen because one of Saul's servants "happened" to know that he knew how to play the harp beautifully. Although he was probably only a teenager, and although he was the youngest son, and although he was "just" a shepherd, evidently he hadn't been wasting those long hours on the rocky fields around Bethlehem. He had gained a reputation as a gifted musician *and* a brave warrior—two qualities much admired in ancient Israel. Therefore, his father sent him to serve Saul, who liked him immediately. The rest is history. His music gave him an introduction to the leaders of Israel. Not long after that, he defeated Goliath, which meant he would never again be a lowly shepherd.

He was ready when his opportunity came, and he made the most of it. None of us orchestrate how or when our opportunity will come. But we can do something about being ready.

Find your passion. Sharpen your skills. Pay the price

to be the best you can be. Take care of your part and God will take care of what happens next.

> *Spirit of God, help me to do my job well today so that I will be ready when my ship comes in. Amen.*

What are the passions of your life? What are you doing to increase your skill level in each area?

Are you willing to wait for God to promote you to the next level?

FEAR OF THE LORD

---✦---

Where Knowledge Begins

The fear of the Lord is the beginning of knowledge.
Proverbs 1:7*a*

The most important word in this verse is *beginning.* It has three meanings: (1) that which is first in order of priorities; (2) the essence or central truth of something; (3) the capstone, or the crowning achievement, of something. What is the fear of the Lord? It is not cringing in terror. It is respecting God for who He is. It is understanding that God is God and you are not. Those who fear the Lord bow their knees before almighty God and acknowledge that He made the world and runs it according to His plan. Respect for God is where knowledge begins, where knowledge continues, and where all knowledge ends.

Let's consider three implications of this truth. *First, the road of wisdom leads to a temple, not to a palace.* It leads back to God. If your learning leads you away from God, you're learning the wrong things. If your learning leads you toward greater independence from God and His Word, you have been studying at the feet of the wrong teachers. All true learning begins with the understanding that there is a God to whom all of us must one day give an account.

Second, all education that leaves God out omits the central principle of the universe. Suppose a high school teacher stood up on the first day of class and said, "Because I am a Christian, I am going to teach you from the standpoint of the Christian faith. I am going to let my Christian faith influence all of my instruction. I am going to be up front about it. You don't have to believe what I believe, but I am not going to hide my Christian faith. Everything I teach you—whether it's math or geography or algebra or English or world history—will start from the standpoint of the Christian faith because I believe that the fear of the Lord is the beginning of knowledge." How long would that teacher last? Yet any education that doesn't begin precisely at that point can hardly be called education at all, for the fear of the Lord is the foundation of all true learning.

Third, education without God produces intellectual giants and moral pygmies. Chuck Colson is right. When you take God away from the educational system, what you get is chaos. No crime bill, no educational bill, no bureaucratic solution can solve that problem until we come back to what God said three thousand years ago: "The fear of the Lord is the beginning of knowledge." If you have four advanced degrees but don't have the fear of the Lord, you would be better off as an undeducated reader of the Bible who at least believes in God. I am in favor of education that bows the knee to Jesus Christ. If you have to make a choice, choose the fear of the Lord, for without it you're still in spiritual kindergarten.

Spirit of Truth, help me to know God so that through Him I might understand the universe He created. Amen.

Do you "fear the Lord"? What does that phrase mean to you?

How can Christian students and faculty members take their faith with them into the public school system?

FLEXIBILITY

✦

Shifting Gears Without Changing Direction

Many are the plans in a man's heart, but it is the Lord's purpose that prevails.

Proverbs 19:21

Flexibility is the ability to adjust to a changing situation. Some people are naturally better at this than others, but all of us need some degree of flexibility, for we live in world of change.

My wife happened to hear a fascinating comment on the radio while we were cutting across the edge of Georgia on our way from Tallahassee, Florida, to Dothan, Alabama. She scribbled it down so I could look at it later. "The key to success in life is how well you adapt to Plan B."

There is a world of truth in that simple sentence. So many of us go through life frustrated because we're still working on Plan A. That's the one where everything works out, where your marriage lasts forever, where your children grow up without any problems, where you climb to the top of the career ladder, where everyone loves you and no one hates you, where all your dreams come true and you live happily ever after.

Unfortunately, Plan A never pans out. Life isn't that

simple or that easy. Meanwhile, the people who are frustrated by the failure of Plan A are overtaken by the folks who have decided to make Plan B work instead.

What's Plan B? It's the reality that your divorce is final and your marriage is over. It's the reality that your first career choice was a mistake and now it's time to start over. It's the reality that you don't have the money to buy the bigger house you want. It's the truth that you have cancer and your future is uncertain. It's the understanding that some people who seemed to be close friends aren't going to be there for you when you really need them. It's the reality that you lost the election even though you were clearly the better candidate.

Born in poverty and educated at home, he failed in his first business venture, ran for office the next year and was defeated, failed in yet another business, had a nervous breakdown, and was defeated in five more elections. But he never gave up, and in 1860 Abraham Lincoln was elected president.

Plan A not working out for you? Don't despair. Plan A *never* works out. Your success in life is largely determined by how well you adapt to Plan B.

Here are two suggestions for those who feel a bit overwhelmed by circumstances: *First, embrace change as a natural part of life.* Solomon says as much when he writes, "There is a time for everything, and a season for every activity under heaven" (Ecclesiastes 3:1). If you live long enough, you'll eventually see it all—birth and death, war and peace, building up and tearing down, winning and losing, loving and hating. Nothing stays the same. You can fight change, but you can't stop it.

Second, embrace the only Person who never changes. "Jesus Christ is the same yesterday and today and forever" (Hebrews 13:8). Leaders come and go; children are born, grow up, and die. But Jesus Christ never changes! He remains the same. He is the one constant in an ever-changing world. Anchor your life in Him and you can face the future without fear.

> *Lord Jesus, You are the still point in our turning world. Help us to find our security in You alone. Amen.*

What was the Plan A of your life? How well are you doing on Plan B?

How well do you embrace change? How can a person who loves order and regularity learn to grow more flexible?

FORGIVENESS

❖

Letting Go of the Past

A man's wisdom gives him patience; it is to his glory to over-look an offense.

Proverbs 19:11

Many Christians struggle with issues of anger and bitterness because of things that have happened to them in the past. How do we find freedom from those angry feelings? May I remind you of two truths? First, you are to forgive because God has already forgiven you. Ephesians 4:32 says, "Be kind and compassionate to one another, forgiving each other, just as in Christ God forgave you." Second, you are to forgive because you promised God you would forgive. Every time you pray the Lord's Prayer you are promising to forgive. "Forgive us our debts as we also have forgiven our debtors."

As long as you hold a grudge, you are chained to the past. As long as you are angry about the way you have been treated, you are still living in the past.

Recently a friend made a statement that stuck in my mind. Out of the blue, she said, "I have decided to forgive him." No conditions, just a simple declaration of intent. That strikes me as an entirely Christian thing to do. We choose to forgive even when some part of us would rather hold a grudge.

The most important truth to know is that forgiveness is an act of the heart. You forgive by a conscious choice of your will. For those who have been deeply hurt, forgiveness means consciously choosing not to dwell in the past, not to constantly repeat the sordid story of what was done to you. It means actively deciding you will move forward by faith, letting go of the bitter feelings one by one.

This isn't easy, and it won't happen overnight, and you will probably need the help of some good friends who can help you talk through your feelings and hold you accountable to move forward and not backward. But it can be done.

In one of her books, Corrie ten Boom tells of some Christian friends who wronged her in a public and malicious way. For many days, she was bitter and angry until she forgave them. But in the night she would wake up thinking about what they had done and she would get angry all over again. It seemed the memory would not go away.

Help came from her Lutheran pastor to whom she confessed her frustration after two sleepless weeks. He told her, "Corrie, up in the church tower is a bell which is rung by pulling on a rope. When the sexton pulls the rope, the bells peal out—ding-dong, ding-dong, ding-dong. But if he doesn't keep pulling on the rope, the sound slowly fades away. *Forgiveness is like that. When we forgive someone, we take our hand off the rope.* But if we've been tugging at our grievances for a long time, we mustn't be surprised if the old angry thoughts keep coming for a while. They are just the ding-dongs of the old bell slowing down."

So it's not surprising if, after forgiveness, the memories keep coming back for a while. If you refuse to dwell on them, slowly they will fade away. Why? *When you forgive, you let go of the rope and the force is gone out of your anger.*

> *Lord Jesus, You showed us how to forgive those who hurt us. Help me to do that, I pray. Amen.*

What are the major forgiveness issues in your life right now? What needs to happen in each case so you can "let go of the rope"?

Do you have a friend with whom you can talk over these forgiveness issues?

FRIENDSHIP

The Bridge over Troubled Waters

A friend loves at all times, and a brother is born for adversity.
Proverbs 17:17

To know and be known, to love and be loved, to care and be cared for—these are our deepest human needs. That means having a few people gathered around who know you through and through. That means knowing others deeply and intimately, and it means letting them get to know you in the same way.

There is nothing more important I can say to you than this statement: *God never intended that you should live the Christian life by yourself.* He intended that the Christian life should not be a solo, but a duet, a trio, a quartet, a quintet, a choir, and a mighty symphony. He intended that as you join your life with other people, they would help you and you would help them.

How is it with you? Do you have a few people in your life who really know you? Or do you always wear the mask and the costume and play the game "because the show must go on"? Are you accountable to anybody for the way you live? Or are you just doing it all by yourself?

One reason you may be struggling right now is that you don't have a group, and you're not close to anyone, and you're not accountable to anybody. God never intended that His children would live like hermits. He intended that they would live together, and that in living together, they would help each other along the way. It is God's will that we live together as brothers and sisters in a family relationship so that we can love each another, encourage each other, admonish each other, hug each other, pick each other up when we fall down, rejoice together, weep together, and correct each other when we make mistakes.

But when the chips are down, and the world is falling apart, and your plans have come to nothing, you soon discover the difference between acquaintances and friends. True friends stay with you when the going gets rough. Do you have any friends to whom you can unburden your heart, knowing that they will not be shocked, no matter what you say? Do you have anyone in your life with whom you can share the deepest secrets of your heart? Are you a friend like that to anyone else?

Do you have anyone in your life to whom you can spill the beans—the good with the bad, the ugly with the beautiful—knowing that you are completely safe because they will keep the good and forget about the bad? How blessed you are if the answer is yes; how lonely you must be if the answer is no.

God never intended you to go through life all alone. He never intended that you should face your problems by yourself. There is hardly a problem we couldn't solve if we decided to face our problems together. There is hardly a difficulty we couldn't overcome if we decided to be honest with each other.

O God, teach me what it means to love deeply and pro-foundly, as Jesus did. Amen.

Who are your five closest friends? Do you have trouble letting people get close to you?

In your mind, what is the most important quality a good friend should possess?

GENEROSITY

❖

What Size Is Your Shovel?

A generous man will prosper; he who refreshes others will himself be refreshed.

Proverbs 11:25

The blessings of generosity are mentioned several times in the book of Proverbs. Those who honor the Lord with their wealth will find their barns filled to overflowing (3:9–10), and the generous will be blessed (22:9), especially those who give to the poor (19:17). In essence, God is saying, "If you give to the poor (who can't return the favor), it's as if you gave it to Me personally, and I will see that you are repaid."

Generous giving is not difficult when we understand that everything we have comes from God. *This is the basic truth that animates all Christian giving.* All that we are and all that we have comes from God. Everything is a gift. Nothing is earned; everything is given.

You own nothing. *Everything you have is on loan from God.* He gives it to you for a little while and says, "Take care of it." We hold on tight because we think it all belongs to us. Sooner or later we'll understand that it doesn't belong to us—and it never did.

What do you do when you're running short on money but see a need and you want to get involved? I think the answer is clear. *You give whatever you can and trust God to take care of you.* It may not be a lot. Indeed, it may be very small. The amount doesn't matter. What matters is the attitude of the heart.

God specifically promises to take care of generous givers. And He promises to give back to you in accordance with the measure of generosity you use in your giving in the first place. Jesus specifically made that promise in Luke 6:38: "Give, and it will be given to you. A good measure, pressed down, shaken together and running over, will be poured into your lap. For with the measure you use, it will be measured to you." My friend Howard Harvey calls this the Shovel Principle: "I shovel it out and God shovels it in, and He's got a bigger shovel than I do."

I like that because it perfectly catches the spirit of Jesus' words. Generous givers are not the people with a large bank account, but the people with a large view of God. We often look at people who give generously and think, "They must be rich." But it is not so. *Poor people are often very generous, and rich people can be very stingy.* Generosity has nothing to do with how much money you have. But it has everything to do with your view of God.

If your God is big, you will be generous. If He is small, you will be stingy. *If you struggle with your giving, it may be because your God is too small.* The bigger your God, the easier it will be for you to give.

Someone has said that since we can't take it with us, the best thing we can do with our money is to give it away. I have a feeling that Solomon (who was an extremely rich man) would agree with that thought. God takes care of generous givers. You may not get rich by giving your money away, but you'll never know as long as you keep it all for yourself.

Lord God, open my eyes to see how much You have given me and how rich I already am. Amen.

How big is your God? How does your view of God impact your giving?

Do you really believe what Jesus says in Luke 6:38?

GENTLENESS

※

Power Under Control

A gentle answer turns away wrath, but a harsh word stirs up anger.

Proverbs 15:1

I have a friend who learned this verse the hard way. Whenever she said something in a harsh tone, her mother made her write this verse fifty times on a sheet of paper. It must have worked, for many years later she has no trouble recalling the verse.

But putting them into practice is a challenge for all of us. Many an argument has started because someone spoke the truth in an angry tone. With that in mind, here is a simple three-word definition of gentleness: *Power under control.*

A survey of the New Testament shows how important this virtue is. Galatians 5:22–23 lists gentleness as one of the fruits of the Spirit. Colossians 3:12 includes it as part of the "clothing" of the Christian. James 1:19–21 tells us that meekness is the opposite of anger and moral filth. It is the basic attitude we are to have toward all people (Philippians 4:5), especially those who oppose us (2 Timothy 2:24–26). By a gentle and quiet spirit a Christian wife may win her unbelieving husband (1 Peter 3:1–6).

That leads me to suggest an expanded definition of

gentleness. *Gentleness is self-control displayed in a calm spirit based on an unshakable confidence in God.* It is self-control based on God's control. Thus, it is truly a supernatural virtue produced by the Holy Spirit.

Consider Jesus. He was the most powerful man who ever lived—and yet His power was always under His Father's control. He got angry when he chased the money changers out of the temple—but He never lost His temper. He rebuked the Pharisees—but ate with prostitutes and tax collectors. He welcomed children and spoke to large crowds—but felt the touch of a woman whose fingers brushed the hem of His garment.

This Jesus was no effeminate sissy. He could raise the dead, cast out demons, and calm a stormy sea. Yet the Bible says that "as a sheep before her shearers is dumb, so he openeth not his mouth" (Isaiah 53:7, KJV). He didn't debate Pilate, He didn't curse Herod, and He didn't fight the soldiers. As the old gospel song says, He could have called ten thousand angels, but He died alone for you and me.

That's true gentleness. Ultimate power under God's control. He was the Son of God who made others feel welcome around Him. When people came to Him, they felt rested, not harassed or pressured. No wonder the common people loved Him.

Gentleness is that quality which is best demonstrated when you are dealing with unreasonable people. It is seen when you are under the gun, up against a deadline, surrounded by problems, hip deep in alligators and no way to drain the swamp, and you feel yourself getting frustrated. If you don't have it then, you just don't have it at all.

The gentle man does not fight for his own rights, does not insist upon personal vindication, does not always have to correct others, does not repay in kind, does not return insult for insult, and does not use force and intimidation to get his way.

No one can consistently live this way apart from the grace of God. The good news is, God has plenty of grace, even for the worst moments of life. All you have to do is ask Him for it.

Lord Jesus, teach me the strength of gentleness and the wisdom of kindness. Amen.

Are you a gentle person? How would your friends answer that question? If you don't know the answer, why not ask them yourself?

How do you personally balance gentleness with the need to be bold in the face of evil?

GOSSIP

Feathers in the Wind

The words of a gossip are like choice morsels; they go down to a man's inmost parts.

Proverbs 18:8

Here are a few verses to ponder: "He who conceals his hatred has lying lips, and whoever spreads slander is a fool" (10:18). "A perverse man stirs up dissension, and a gossip separates close friends" (16:28). "A gossip betrays a confidence; so avoid a man who talks too much" (20:19).

Once upon a time a man said something about his neighbor that was untrue. The word spread around the village as one person told another. But soon the truth came out—what could the man do? He went to see the village priest, and the priest gave him some strange instructions.

"Take a bag full of feathers and place one feather on the doorstep of each person who heard the untrue story you told. Then go back a day later, pick up the feathers, and bring the bag back to me."

So the man did as the priest, said. But when he went back to pick up the feathers, nearly all of them were gone. When he went back to the priest, he said, "Father, I did as you said but when I went back the wind had blown the feathers away and I could not get them back." And the

priest replied, "So it is with careless w
they are spoken, they cannot be take
forgiveness for what you said, but yo
words back. The damage has already b

So it is with gossip. "Hey, did yo
Tom did?" "Let me tell you what Ph ——— me, I
just heard Susan and George are separating. Can you believe it?" "Jay is about to lose his job—he's been goofing
off again." "Ethel finally talked Lloyd into buying a new
car. And you know how Lloyd is about money." And on
and on it goes.

It's not just that we play fast and loose with the truth.
Sometimes we tell 80 percent of the truth and conve-
niently forget part of the story. Sometimes we tell all the
truth we know, but the part we don't know changes the
whole picture. Sometimes we tell the truth but in such a
way as to make someone look stupid. Sometimes we just
plain lie.

Anyway you slice it, it's gossip. And it's hurtful. And
it's wrong. And God hates it. And we should too.

There is an easy cure. But it takes tremendous discipline. Keep your mouth shut. It works every time.

If you must share what you know, use three questions
as guides before telling what you know to someone else.

Is it true?

Is it kind?

Is it necessary?

There wouldn't be any gossip if we used these three
questions before speaking.

Spirit of Truth, Holiness, and Love, fill us with Your divine presence that our words may reflect the character of Jesus. Amen.

How do you define gossip? How often are you guilty of spreading gossip? What changes do you need to make in this area of your life?

GUIDANCE

❖

Higher Hands Are Leading Me

In his heart a man plans his course, but the Lord determines his steps.

Proverbs 16:9

Proverbs 16:9 is one of the most profound verses in all the Bible. It is both a promise and a warning. You make your plans, but God determines which way you're going to go.

Often God's guidance comes through suddenly changing circumstances. Have you ever had that happen to you? You had your life all planned out. You were going *this* way. You were convinced that God's will was *this* way. Then the phone call came that changed the course of your life. Or the boss called you in and said, "We're downsizing. Your job has been eliminated." Or the letter came that said, "You are an excellent candidate, but unfortunately our incoming class is full." Or you asked her to marry you, "knowing" it was the will of God, but she hadn't discovered it yet—and said no. The investment you counted on for retirement didn't come through. You get cancer. When these troubles occur, we think something has gone wrong in the universe. God has made a mistake. This *couldn't* have happened this way.

Please read the next sentence carefully. *What you call*

circumstance is really the sovereign hand of God in your life. Every circumstance that comes into your life, whether good or bad—all of them together have come down to you from the good and gracious hand of God. They are all ultimately for your benefit and for His glory.

Proverbs 16:9 tells us that it didn't happen by chance. It never does for the people of God. Who is it that opens the doors? It's God! Who is it that shuts the doors? It's God! Who gives opportunities? It's God! Who takes them away? It's God! He is the One who is in charge.

While rummaging through an accumulated mountain of mail, I came across an article about "the prevenient grace of God." The phrase—which was new to me—refers to "the grace that goes before." Here's a working definition: "In every situation of life God is already at work *before* I get there. He is working creatively, strategically, and redemptively for my good and His glory."

So many times I tend to limit my thinking to the fact that God's presence goes with me as I go through life. That's true, but it's only part of the story. He's not only with me now, He's already way up the road ahead of me.

Or to say it another way: *While I'm living in Tuesday, He's clearing the road for me on Friday.* Or to say it yet another way: *God is already at work providing solutions for problems I don't even know I have yet.*

Are you worried about next week? Forget it. He's already there. How about next year? Don't sweat it. He's already there. What about that crucial meeting next week? Sleep well. He's already there. What about that tough decision that looms ahead of you? Fear not. He's already there.

It would be enough if God simply walked with you through the events of life. But He does much more than that. He goes ahead of you, clearing the way, arranging the details of life, so that when you get there, you can have confidence that He has already been there before you.

That's the prevenient grace of God. He goes before His people. He's at work in the future while we live in the present.

Thank you, Lord, for taking charge of the details of my life. Amen.

When was the last time an unexpected circumstance changed your life? How can you see God's hand in that situation?

What are your greatest worries right now? Are you willing to trust God with them?

HARD WORK

✦

The Reason We Get Out of Bed

He who works his land will have abundant food, but he who chases fantasies lacks judgment.

Proverbs 12:11

Hard work yesterday does not guarantee tomorrow's success. Hard work yesterday has to be followed up with hard work today to guarantee tomorrow's prosperity.

Every day you face a choice of going one of two ways. *You can go the easy way or the hard way.* The easy way is the way of procrastination. It is the way of staying in bed when the alarm clock goes off. The easy way is the way of saying it doesn't matter whether I work today or not; it doesn't matter what time I show up; it doesn't matter if I check out a few minutes early—the boss isn't around, and, after all, it's good enough for government work. It is the way of no plans, no forethought, no enthusiasm, no diligence. The easy way says take it easy, slow down, back off, don't have a heart attack. It is the soft and cuddly way. It is the way of laziness, the way of the sluggard.

All of us are born on the easy way. A voice inside whispers, "Take a shortcut. Cheat if you have to. Cut some corners. Pull some strings. Take it easy. Don't work too hard. Where's the fire? Slow down, man."

The hard way means getting up early to have your

daily devotions whether you feel like it or not. It involves preparation, long-range planning, goal setting, future orientation, diligence, forethought, showing up for work on time, giving eight hours of work for eight hours of pay, doing what you're told and then doing what needs to be done, even if you're not told. It means paying the price to cross racial lines for the sake of Jesus Christ. The man who takes the hard way doesn't send his children to church; he takes them with him. He sacrifices time out with his buddies so he can spend time with his wife. The hard way means putting God's kingdom ahead of your own interests, even at the expense of career advancement. If you decide to go the hard way, you're going to have to get in shape mentally, physically, socially, emotionally, and spiritually.

Here's an important insight that many men never discover: *God is on the hard road. He's not sitting with the couch potatoes.* The hard road looks difficult and daunting. All of us would rather be on the easy road. God is calling you to stop making excuses and get in the ball game.

Do you want to know the ironic thing about the easy road and the hard road? *The easy road looks easy, but once you get on it, it turns into the hard road. And the hard road looks hard, but once you do the hard thing in life, it turns out to be the easy road.* The easy road is deceptive. It is the way of destruction, poverty, starvation, and desperation. It is the way to wasted days, wasted weeks, wasted months, and wasted years. The hard road that appears to be so difficult is ultimately the road of blessing, fulfill-ment, and lasting spiritual growth. It is the road that leads you to the top. The easy road takes you down to the bottom. Smart people take the hard road and end up smiling, while the folks on the easy road can only dream of what might have been.

> *Lord God, give me the courage and the discipline to stay on the hard road today. Amen.*

How do you spot a person on the "hard road"? the "easy road"?

What is the "hard road" for you personally, and what is your version of the "easy road"?

Which road are you traveling right now?

HEART

✦

Where Life Makes Up Its Mind

Above all else, guard your heart, for it is the wellspring of life.

Proverbs 4:23

The term *heart* in the Bible generally refers to the innermost part of life. It is the decision-making center, the source of motives, the seat of the passions, and the center of the conscience. It is truly the place "where life makes up its mind."

Proverbs has a great deal to say about the heart. It is the source of wisdom (2:10) and understanding (8:5, KJV), the origin of both deceit (6:14) and joy (15:30). The heart may backslide (14:14, KJV) or trust in God (3:5). It may be cheerful (15:13), prideful (16:5), bitter (14:10), haughty (18:12), or prudent (18:15, KJV). The heart may lust after an adulterous woman (6:25), rage against the Lord (19:3), and eventually be hardened against God altogether (28:14). The Lord tests the heart (17:3) because He knows what is in it (24:12), which is why the heart must be guarded all the time (4:23).

Jesus almost certainly had this verse in mind when He spoke to the Pharisees in Matthew 12:34*b*: "For out of the overflow of the heart the mouth speaks." This verse cuts both ways. Whatever is on the inside will eventually come out—whether good or bad (v. 35). If a person's heart is dirty, he cannot produce purity in his life. Likewise, if the heart is stayed on the Lord, it will be seen on the outside eventually. The King James Version of Proverbs 23:7 reads, "As [a man] thinketh in his heart, so is he."

- If you think angry thoughts, angry words are sure to follow.
- If you fill your mind with sexual fantasies, your body will find a way to fulfill those desires.
- If you dwell on your problems, they will soon overwhelm you.
- If you feel like a victim, soon you will become one.
- If you give way to worry, don't be surprised when you get ulcers.
- If you focus on how others misunderstand you, you will soon become angry and bitter.

What goes in must come out. Sooner or later your thoughts translate into reality. You're not what you think you are, but what you think, you are.

The flip side is also true.

- If you focus on the truth, you will speak the truth.
- If you look on noble things, nobility will mark your life.
- If you seek out lovely things, your life will be lovely to others.
- If you dwell on the right, the wrong will seem less attractive to you.

- If you look for virtue, you will find it.
- If you search for higher things, you will elevate your own life.

Recently a friend sent me this prayer from the Book of Common Prayer. It seems a fitting way to apply the words of Proverbs 4:23.

Almighty God, to you all hearts are open, all desires known, and from you no secrets are hid: Cleanse the thoughts of our hearts by the inspiration of your Holy Spirit, that we may perfectly love you and worthily magnify your Holy Name; through Christ our Lord. Amen.

What words would you use to describe the state of your heart right now?

What has your heart been dwelling on recently? What has that produced in your own life?

HONESTY

✦

The Best Defense for a Bad Memory

An honest answer is like a kiss on the lips.

Proverbs 24:26

This verse will suggest different things to different people. What exactly does it mean, and what is the relationship between an honest answer and a kiss on the lips? I think there are three points of comparison: (1) Just as it is relatively rare to be kissed on the lips, even so it is relatively rare to hear a true and honest answer. (2) Just as a kiss on the lips means more than a kiss on the cheek, even so an honest answer is a mark of true sincerity. (3) Just as a kiss on the lips can be and should be deeply satisfying to the soul, even so an honest answer is satisfying to the soul.

Let's face it. *We live in a cynical age when truth is in short supply.*

- The polls show we don't think our leaders are telling us the truth.
- Our motto seems to be: "Tell the truth as long as it is convenient."
- When an election rolls around, it's open season on the truth.
- One campaign has a "Truth Squad"; the other has a

"Department of Defense."

• "If you lie about me, I'm going to lie about you."

In the process, truth is first devalued, then lost altogether.

Proverbs 6:16–19 tells us the seven things the Lord hates. Two especially deal with the lack of honesty: a lying tongue and the false witness who pours out lies. Proverbs 14:25 tells us that "a truthful witness saves lives, but a false witness is deceitful." According to Proverbs 12:19, "Truthful lips endure forever, but a lying tongue lasts only a moment."

This week I read about a man who told a lie at work. "I got in trouble and I told a lie to cover up what I had done. But then I found that I needed to tell another lie to cover up for the first lie. But then I had to tell a third lie to cover up the first two lies I told. Then I had to tell another one to cover up the third lie, a fifth lie to cover up the fourth lie, and I kept on until I finally sat down and counted up and realized that I had to tell forty-two lies in a row to cover up for the first one."

Another man was fired from a high-level executive job. The reason was simple: lying, bending the truth. It wasn't out-and-out scheming as much as ignored opportunity to come clean. When challenged, he covered up and was discovered. He was the company's rising star—personally changing the face of a multimillion-dollar business. He lost his job because he couldn't tell the truth.

If you lose your money, you can always make some more. If you lose your integrity, you may never get it back.

Tell the truth the first time and you won't have to worry about having a bad memory.

Spirit of Truth, create in me a love for the truth and a holy hatred for lying. Make me an honest person in all my dealings. Amen.

Have you ever lost a position or been punished in any way for dishonesty? How did that affect you? Do you consider yourself (a) scrupulously honest, (b) mostly honest, (c) honest when it counts, or (d) honest when it is convenient?

How can a person who struggles in this take steps toward honesty?

HONOR

Winning the Respect of Others

A man's pride brings him low, but a man of lowly spirit gains honor.

Proverbs 29:23

Here we have a double prediction. Pride destroys, but humility brings honor. In the first category are many examples. For instance, King Nebuchadnezzar lost his mind and was made to eat grass like the cattle. For seven years his body "was drenched with the dew of heaven until his hair grew like the feathers of an eagle and his nails like the claws of a bird" (Daniel 4:33). This startling transformation took place because he was proud and took credit for his own accomplishments, refusing to give God the glory. God brought him down in the most humiliating way possible. If he had died it would not have been as shocking as the sight of the mightiest man on earth looking like a wild animal and romping in the field with cattle.

But this strange story is also instructive in a positive way. Daniel 4:34 tells us that when the king lifted his eyes toward heaven, his sanity was restored. Then he "honored and glorified him who lives forever." As a result of this change of heart, the king reported, "My honor and splendor were returned to me for the glory of my kingdom" (v.

36*a*). He was restored to his throne with even greater power than before. His final words are instructive: "Those who walk in pride he [God] is able to humble" (v. 37*b*).

This brings us back to Proverbs 29:23, which links a lowly spirit with honor. Derek Kidner notes that pride is destructive because it opposes the first principle of wisdom—the fear of the Lord. When a man thinks too highly of himself, he is a fitting candidate for God's judgment. To use a modern phrase, the proud man is a sitting duck. By the same token, honor comes to those who admit they don't deserve it.

Proverbs 25:27 flips this concept over when it reminds us, "Nor is it honorable to seek one's own honor." What a rebuke to the modern spirit of self-promotion and "looking out for number one." God delights to reverse the judgments of the world. He chooses the weak to overcome the strong and the foolish to defeat the wise. In the same way, the first shall be last and the last shall be first; those who try to save their lives will lose them, and those who lose their lives in the service of Christ will ultimately find them.

Recently a letter arrived from a missionary friend newly arrived in a foreign land. After speaking of the understandable homesickness and the sense of dislocation, she writes, "There is the calm assurance that this is where we're supposed to be (most days, that is)"—with a little smiley-face at the end of the sentence. That seems to be a wonderfully balanced approach to the challenges she and her husband face. Later she mentions the joy that comes from being where the Lord wants her to be "even when I don't feel happy to be here."

Is this not what it means to "find" your soul by losing it? Honor comes to those who day by day humble themselves and do God's will, whatever it may be.

Lord Jesus, help me today to do Your will and trust You for the results. Amen.

Do you know anyone whose pride led to his downfall? When you think of humility, whose name comes to mind? What kind of honor has that person received?

As far as you know it, what is God's will for you today?

HOPE

---❖---

Future-Tense Living

Do not let your heart envy sinners, but always be zealous for the fear of the Lord. There is surely a future hope for you, and your hope will not be cut off.

Proverbs 23:17–18

Envy makes sense if this world is all there is; it makes no sense at all if there is another world to come. If you believe you have "future hope," you won't waste time envying sinners, for their present prosperity won't last forever. Soon enough, they will be judged, but those who fear the Lord have a "future hope" that can never be cut off. In the meantime, believers are to look up to the Lord and look ahead to the promised reward.

The word *hope* in Hebrew means first to wait, then to wait expectantly. The concept is very close to our English word *confidence*. An expanded definition would be "to wait on something because you know that the thing you are waiting for will happen because the person you are waiting on is trustworthy."

You have a choice to make. Either you choose to live like everyone else or you choose to wait on the Lord. What credit is it if you trust God because you have a mate, a house, a job, a happy home, a secure future, and good health? What will you do when you lose your mate, your job, your home, your family, your security, your reputation, your connections, and your health? When life tumbles in, what then?

That's what hope is all about. It's choosing to put your confidence in God alone. It's believing that He has answers to questions you can barely understand. It's coming to the place where you don't measure your spirituality by your prosperity. It's finding rest in your soul because you discover that the things you used to crave aren't so important anymore.

I think it's important to remember that this hope has both a present and a future component. In Mark 10:29–30, Jesus reminded His disciples that "no one who has left home or brothers or sisters or mother or father or children or fields for me and the gospel will fail to receive a hundred times as much in this present age (homes, brothers, sisters, mothers, children and fields—and with them, persecutions) and in the age to come, eternal life." God will be no one's debtor. Even in this life, even amid suffering and persecution, we will still find that it was worthwhile to follow Jesus. That's an important perspective to keep in mind when we see the wicked apparently prospering while the righteous are overlooked. But our blessing is a hundredfold greater because we know the Lord and the wicked don't. And we are surrounded by fellow believers who are like family to us.

Don't worry about evildoers. Let them enjoy their little moment in the sun. And don't waste a moment wishing you could be like them. Put your hope in the

Lord and keep on moving ahead. We've got it better now, and this is only the beginning.

Father, forgive us for doubting Your promises about the future. Help us to live in the light of eternity. Amen.

Name four ways the wicked prosper today. List several reasons that God doesn't judge them right now.

Can you think of an area of your life where you are being forced to put your trust in God alone?

HUMILITY

✦

The Way Up Is Down

When pride comes, then comes disgrace, but with humility comes wisdom.

Proverbs 11:2

It's always tricky to talk about humility. How do you know when you're truly humble? Come to think of it, if you are truly humble, will you even know it? Humility is the virtue which, when you think you have it, you've lost it.

It's helpful to know that the Hebrew word for "proud" is related to the Hebrew word for "high." In the Old Testament, it was used for high trees and high mountains. It was used to describe King Saul, who stood higher than anyone else in Israel. It was also used of God, who was said to be "on high" and whose thoughts are higher than the thoughts of man. We use the word in the same way when we say, "Get off your high horse, buster."

We live in a culture that puts a very low value on humility. They don't give out merit badges for humility. From the moment we enter the world we are urged to get ahead, to climb the ladder, to "look out for number one," to win through intimidation, and to prove our success by the car we drive, the home we buy, the clothes we wear, and the friends we keep.

Humility in this context simply means that you don't run the world, you don't have all the answers, you know your limits. That last one is a hard one for some people—the idea that you have limits. It's sort of a trendy, New Age–type idea to talk about unlimited potential and the untapped resources within. The truth is, our potential is very limited and the only untapped resources are the ones we discover when we come to the end and admit that we are limited but God is not.

What is humility? *It's having a right view of yourself because you have a right view of God.* Humility does *not* mean saying, "I'm a nothing, I'm a worm, I'm useless." That's not humility; that's self-pity, which is really another form of pride.

And what is pride? *It's having too large a view of yourself because you have too small a view of God.* When your God is big, you will be small and pride will be impossible.

This is humility: "God made me and I belong to Him. Every good thing I have in life is a gift from the Almighty. Some have more, some have less. It matters not to me. I thank God for what I have, and I'm going to do the best I can with what God has given me, and I'm going to leave the outcome with Him."

If we live that way, it will save us so much trouble. We won't have to get into a power game at work or live in the rat race or sell our convictions to get ahead. We won't get angry at the silly comments people make. Humility enables us to be who we are in Christ. And we won't have to worry about what others think.

Humble me, Lord, lest I should think more of myself than I ought and block Your power in my life. Amen.

Name three people you would call humble. What qualities do they have in common?

Why is self-pity just another form of pride?

INITIATIVE

No More Excuses

Do not withhold good from those who deserve it, when it is in your power to act. Do not say to your neighbor, "Come back later; I'll give it tomorrow"—when you now have it with you.

Proverbs 3:27–28

Here is a warning against procrastination in well doing. It is a clarion call for doing good *today*—not tomorrow or some other time in the distant future. How easy it is for all of us to be great *intenders*. We intend to be generous, we plan to be kind, we even dream about the good things we would do if we ever won a million dollars.

But God is less concerned about the million you might someday have than He is with the twenty dollars in your pocket right now. By the same token, you can't help the poor, visit the sick, or lift up the fallen by putting these tasks off until tomorrow. As James 4:13–17 reminds us, how do you even know if you will be alive tomorrow? Or what if you lose your money in the meantime?

Life is uncertain. When asked how he wanted to be remembered, noted radio commentator Paul Harvey replied, "I want to be remembered as a man who left the woodpile a little higher than when he found it." That's a noble goal, but it won't happen by accident and you can't wait till the end of life to start stacking that wood. You have to pick up a few logs each day.

Galatians 6:2 says, "Carry each other's burdens, and in this way you will fulfill the law of Christ." When you help someone with his burden, your own burden grows lighter. When you reach out a helping hand to someone else, the Lord makes the way easier for you. So many of us are a little too inward-focused, a little too myopic, looking at ourselves. Write down the names of at least three people who have a burden you could help carry this week. Maybe you could give them a call, write them a letter, give them some money, give them a hug, go to see them, help them with a project, bake them some cookies or food, or spend some time with them. Instead of focusing on your own problems, think about carrying a burden for someone else. Ask the Lord to show you who you could help this week.

Oh, I know the excuses we make. "Let somebody else do it." "Let them get a job and earn some money." "I don't want to think about it." "Who cares, anyway?" "Nobody ever gave me anything." "You're just trying to make me feel guilty."

Hear the Word of the Lord:

> When you give a luncheon or dinner, do not invite your friends, your brothers or relatives, or your rich neighbors; if you do, they may invite you back and so you will be repaid. But when you give a banquet, in-

vite the poor, the crippled, the lame, the blind, and you will be blessed. Although they cannot repay you, you will be repaid at the resurrection of the righteous. (Luke 14:12–14)

What are you doing in a practical way to help the poor, the needy, the hurting, and the hopeless? Before you answer, just remember three little words. *No more excuses.*

Lord, stop me in my tracks so that I won't insult You with more excuses for not doing what You have told me to do. Amen.

Name someone you know who is consistently involved with helping others in need. Would anyone list you as a good example in this area? Why or why not?

Name a situation where you are making some inward excuses for not getting involved. What should you do about it?

INSIGHT

✦

A Time to Answer
and a Time to Walk Away

Do not answer a fool according to his folly, or you will be like him yourself. Answer a fool according to his folly, or he will be wise in his own eyes.

Proverbs 26:4–5

Critics have sometimes seized on these verses as proof that the Bible contradicts itself. But a moment's reflection shows how absurd that is. The very fact that these verses are put back-to-back proves that they are not meant to contradict each other. Rather, the writer put them together to press home an important point. Sometimes you answer a fool; sometimes you don't. What you do depends on the person you're talking to.

In some cases, answering a fool will cause you to be lowered to his level. Oftentimes someone will offer an argument simply to hear the sound of his own voice. Or perhaps someone will engage you in an argument with no other purpose than to cause you to lose your temper. The wise person senses when the motive is other than a fair-minded search for the truth and doesn't bother to enter the fray. He simply walks away. Better to say nothing than to descend to the level of gutter talk.

Other times, if you don't answer him, he'll simply conclude that you don't have an answer and thus will become "wise in his own conceit." This often happens in discussing issues relating to apologetics. Sometimes you simply must open your mouth and defend the truth that the Bible is God's Word, that Jesus Christ is the Son of God, that this world did not evolve but was created by the hand of God, that there is such a thing as absolute morality, that there is no salvation outside of Jesus Christ.

Are not these propositions controversial? Indeed they are. But by responding you are providing reasons for the hope that is within you (1 Peter 3:15). And the Lord may use your answer to win your adversary (2 Timothy 2:24–26). At the very least, you will have given him food for thought. Perhaps the seeds you plant will bring forth a harvest of eternal life.

I have a simple rule I follow for deciding whether or not to enter a discussion. If it's a personal issue with me, I walk away. That is, if I feel myself needing to win an argument instead of persuading another person, then for me it's time to back off. The same thing applies if I feel myself getting angry at the other person.

Perhaps the Lord Jesus is the best example of both proverbs. When He stood before the high priest, Jesus refused to answer the false charges brought against Him (Matthew 26:62–63). But when Pilate questioned Him, He readily entered into a dialogue (John 18:28–19:16). One gets the feeling that Jesus sensed Pilate's combination of confusion and curiosity and, therefore, answered his questions.

Ecclesiastes 3 tells us that there is a time for every purpose under heaven, including "a time to be silent and a time to speak" (v. 7). Insight means understanding the difference, sensing the need of the moment, listening carefully, and acting accordingly.

Lord Jesus, grant me the wisdom to know when to speak and when to be silent. Amen.

Have you ever answered a fool only to regret it later? Or have you wished later that you had spoken up instead of remaining silent?

Why did Jesus answer Pilate but not the high priest? What lesson do you draw from that fact? How can we learn the same kind of wisdom?

INTEGRITY

———◆———

The Ultimate Virtue

The man of integrity walks securely, but he who takes crooked paths will be found out.

Proverbs 10:9

The dictionary uses words such as *whole* and *complete* to describe what integrity means. *To borrow a modern expression, a man with integrity "has his act together."* There are no loose ends that threaten his reputation.

Recently I ran across a full-page ad for an international relief organization. The picture shows a young child—perhaps from Central America or possibly Asia—writing at her desk. The ad copy contains the following sentence: "Integrity. It's as simple as being what you say you are." That strikes me as an excellent definition of integrity. It means being what you say you are—*all* the time and in *every* situation.

To be called a man of integrity is the highest possible compliment. Several years ago my older brother took me to visit a cemetery outside Florence, Alabama, near the remains of an antebellum mansion called Forks of Cypress. The mansion was built in the 1820s by James Jackson, an early settler of northwest Alabama. My brother and I walked among the ruins of the mansion and then crossed the country road into the dense forest on the other side. After a quarter mile we found the Jackson family cemetery. There is no sign marking the spot, only a five-foot-high stone wall surrounding about fifty graves. Inside we found a tall marker over James Jackson's grave, with a long inscription extolling his virtues, which were many.

As I walked along, my eyes fastened on the marker for one of his sons, William Moore Jackson. There was his name, the dates 1824–1891, and this simple five-word epitaph: "A man of unquestioned integrity."

Five words to sum up an entire life. Sixty-plus years distilled into five words. But, oh, what truth they tell.

"A man of unquestioned integrity." I cannot think of a better tribute. Then the thought came: What will they put on my tombstone?

At a recent leadership retreat, the speaker hammered away at one point: *A ministry with integrity will stand the test of time.* Everything else fades away—fads come and go, glitz will attract people but it won't hold them, good programs lose their appeal, new buildings grow old, pastors stay for a while and then leave. But integrity never goes out of style. If you have it, people trust you; if you don't, they don't. And if you lose their trust, it's hard to get it back.

We hear a lot these days about family values and the need to rediscover virtue in American society. *The basic building blocks of virtue are actually very simple.* We've known them all along:

Honesty, perseverance, faithfulness, determination, kindness, loyalty, self-control.

We've known these truths since the beginning of time. The problem isn't in the knowing; it's in the doing.

The mind wanders back to a forgotten tombstone and to those five simple words: "A man of unquestioned integrity." The more you think about it, the greater it seems. Five words aren't much to sum up a life of sixty-seven years, but those five will do nicely. In fact, you could do much worse.

I'm not sure what anyone will write on my tombstone. But I wouldn't mind if someone felt I deserved those five words.

Lord, help me to live in such a way that integrity will be one of the first things people think of when they think of me. Amen.

What is your personal definition of integrity? How well do you live up to your own definition?

What would you like to have put on your tombstone as a summary of your life?

INVOLVEMENT

❖

You Can't Pretend You Didn't Know

Rescue those being led away to death; hold back those stag-
gering toward slaughter. If you say, "But we knew nothing
about this," does not he who weighs the heart perceive it?
Does not he who guards your life know it? Will he not repay
each person according to what he has done?

Proverbs 24:11–12

Picture thousands of people being herded into railroad
cars bound for the death camps. None of them will
return. They are heading for mass murder. You are there,
you see it, you know what is happening. What will you
do? It is the Corrie ten Boom question.

Here is a solemn word from the Lord. It's a warning
against those who make excuses for not getting involved.
It's too messy. People won't understand. I can't risk my repu-
tation that way. What if someone sees me? I might get
arrested. It's not my place to say anything. I can't change the
whole world. Why bother trying? On and on you go, arguing against personal involvement. Slowly the train chugs
out of the station. It is too late to do anything now.

This passage is often raised when Christians discuss
their response to the abortion crisis. In this age when
abortion has almost become a national sacrament, it's
good to be reminded that lives are saved and hearts

changed one by one. A moving scene from *Schindler's List* comes to mind. At the end of the film, Oskar Schindler is filled with remorse that he saved so few people. But you saved 1,100, he is reminded. Yet I could have saved more, he cries. Knowing his pain, the survivors present him with a gold ring inscribed with a saying from the Talmud: "Whoever saves one life saves the world entire."

Last year a friend sent me an Advent calendar with the title "Do You Have Room?" It's built around Luke 2:7, "And she gave birth to her firstborn, a son. She wrapped him in cloths and placed him in a manger, because there was no room for them in the inn." As you open the calendar there are tear-off strips of paper containing various contemporary excuses the innkeeper might give today:

"Sorry. It's dinnertime. Don't interrupt me."

"Totally frazzled. I can't handle more company."

"Sorry! Christmas pageant tonight. God bless you. Bye."

"Not now! I'm listening for tonight's Lotto numbers."

"Can't afford to put up company. Sorry."

"Can't. At this point I don't know which end is up."

It was a not-so-subtle reminder that for those who prefer to sit on the sidelines there are always plenty of convenient excuses.

For Corrie ten Boom there really was no option. When she saw the Jews being herded off to the concentration camps, her Christian faith propelled her to action.

One by one she took them in, hiding them in her attic. Eventually the authorities discovered what she was doing and sent her to one of the camps herself. There her sister died, but she lived to tell the story.

When asked why she got involved, she replied very simply, "I had no other choice."

Take a look around you. You can't do everything, but you can do something. If you are a Christian, you have no other choice.

Lord Jesus, You cared enough to get involved in this sinful world. Help me to do the same. Amen.

Name three people you know who got involved in helping others in need.

Where could you make a difference right now? What are you going to do about it?

JUSTICE

✦

The Real American Dream

The righteous care about justice for the poor, but the wicked have no such concern.

Proverbs 29:7

The Pledge of Allegiance ends with these four words: "and justice for all." Every time you say that, you're pledging to be part of a nation that will provide justice for all. And yet I recall the words of Thomas Jefferson who said, "Indeed, I tremble for my country when I remember that God is just."

Is God concerned about justice? If you want to know the answer to that question, just start reading your Bible. You will find the Bible crammed with passages where God expresses His concern for human justice.

The Hebrew word for justice is *mishpat*. Often in the Old Testament this word is applied to God's own character. God is just—He is absolutely fair and righteous in all His dealings. He gives to each person exactly what he deserves. *The command to care about justice means "treating people right because you know God."* In the Bible, this concept is applied in some very concrete ways: caring for the poor; remembering the widows and orphans; not plowing the corners of your field so that the hungry can get food; speaking the truth; paying a fair wage; having honest scales; not cheating; not engaging in extortion; and refusing to take advantage of the less fortunate.

As I read the Old Testament I am struck by what God says about four forgotten groups of people: the widows, the orphans, the poor, and the foreigners. God cares what happens to these four groups of people. By the word *widow*, I have also written down "single parents"; by *orphans*, I have written down "latch-key kids"; by *the poor*, I have written down "the homeless"; and by *foreigners*, I have written down "despised ethnic and racial minorities." It's amazing how relevant God's Word is. If you read any newspaper, you'll find out that the Bible is addressing the very problems that are tearing our society apart.

God sees the displaced peoples of the world. He sees the refugees of the world. He sees the homeless, the hurting of the world, and He cares about them. He wants His people to care about them too.

What does justice look like?

1. Fair play. God tells us not to rig anything or to cheat. He expects us to exercise truth in selling, truth in merchandising, truth in advertising, and fair play toward other people. He requires that there be no favoritism, no pulling of strings, no secret bribes, nothing done under the table or behind closed doors.

2. Fair pay. Jesus condemned the Pharisees for robbing widows' homes. This speaks directly to the slumlords who take advantage of the poor in our major cities.

3. Absolute honesty. That means telling the truth and keeping your promises.

4. Compassion toward the needy. That simply means seeing the need and caring enough to get involved.

When we work for justice, we're truly working for God. Since we live in an unjust world, there is going to be plenty for us to do. We could all be busy twenty-four hours a day and not correct everything. People of justice will rarely be rewarded, for this is an unjust world, but we ought to treat each other fairly anyway.

Stand up for justice, and when you do, God will be standing with you.

Lord Jesus, may I not be ashamed to follow Your lead in standing up for what is right. Amen.

List several examples of injustice you have either seen or personally experienced.

What good things happen when Christians begin to care about justice in the world? What steps could you take in this area?

KINDNESS

The Ministry of Burning Coals

If your enemy is hungry, give him food to eat; if he is thirsty, give him water to drink. In doing this, you will heap burning coals on his head, and the Lord will reward you.

Proverbs 25:21–22

Let's begin by defining who the "enemy" is in this passage. The "enemy" is almost always a friend, a colleague, or a family member who has hurt me in some way. *My enemy by definition will almost always be someone close to me.* Here's a working definition: *An enemy is any person God uses to reveal my weaknesses.* An enemy is like a chisel God uses to chip away at the rough spots in my life. That's why, if you are married, your husband or your wife will be your enemy sometimes. No one knows your weaknesses like your spouse. Spouses know hidden blemishes, secret sins, and bad habits the rest of the world never sees. They know because they live with you every day.

Can a husband be your enemy? Yes, and you can still love him even when you can't stand him. Can a wife be your enemy? Yes, because she constantly, often accidentally, exposes your weaknesses. She sees the real you that no one else ever sees. You may put on a front at church, but your wife knows the real story. Yes, your wife can be your enemy. If she loves you, she'll have to be your enemy from time to time. Otherwise, how are you ever going to get better?

That's why you have to feed your enemy. *You can't let your wife or your husband starve to death.* It wouldn't look good in the newspaper. That's why you have to give your boss or your teacher or that obnoxious person in the next office something to drink. These are people who are close to you, and because they are close to you, God is using them to expose the weak areas of your life.

But there's a happy result from treating your enemies this way. You heap burning coals on their head. Through deeds of love shown to those who have hurt us deeply, we may actually change their hearts. In that case, our enemy has now become our friend.

What would qualify as "hot coals"? A kind word, a phone call, a brief note, a flower, a meal, a small gift, a letter of recommendation, running an errand, offering a ride, helping them complete a project, rewriting their report, stepping in to save a project that was failing, putting in a good word with their superiors, helping them clean the classroom, going bowling with them. *The list is endless, because "hot coals" refers to any act of kindness you do for an enemy.* Your only limit is your creativity.

Then there is the reward: "And the Lord will reward you." But the principle is true, nonetheless. God will be no man's debtor. *God rewards those who show kindness to their enemies.* How will He do it? It's hard to say. One obvious answer might be to cause your "hot coals" to turn your enemy into a friend. Or He might promote you or pour out new blessings or grant you answers to your prayers or give you new spiritual growth.

Not to worry. If you do your part, God will do His. You can count on that.

Father, I confess that it's difficult to love my enemies. And it's even hard to believe You want me to. I need Your help or I'll never be able to do it. Amen.

Name three "enemies" in your life right now. List at least three "hot coals" you can pour on each one.

What kind of "reward" would you like from the Lord in each case?

LEADERSHIP

Paying the Price to Lead the Way

O my son, O son of my womb, O son of my vows, do not spend your strength on women, your vigor on those who ruin kings. It is not for kings, O Lemuel—not for kings to drink wine, not for rulers to crave beer, lest they drink and forget what the law decrees, and deprive all the oppressed of their rights.

Proverbs 31:2–5

There are many verses on leadership in Proverbs. Why choose this passage? Because it points out an often-overlooked truth about leadership in any arena. Since leaders have influence over the lives of others, their responsibility is enormous. Issues that may not matter to others must matter to them. "Like priest, like people" is still true.

During my college years I attended a church pastored by a man who stayed at the church forty-two years. Although he has since retired, he is remembered by those who knew him for one statement, repeated over and over: "Everything rises or falls on leadership."

You could read a thousand books on management and not find a more important principle. In some ways, it is the story of every human endeavor. Every success and every failure can usually be traced back to one ultimate source—

leadership. It matters not whether you are talking about the corner grocery store or a multinational corporation. Leadership makes the difference. It applies just as much to a seven-year-old-boys' soccer team as it does to the New York Yankees. Leadership makes the difference.

The higher you go in leadership, the greater your personal responsibility. James 3:1 seems to say this directly: "Not many of you should presume to be teachers, my brothers, because you know that we who teach will be judged more strictly." That's a very solemn statement. All believers will be judged, but teachers face a stricter judgment. Why? Because they occupy such a powerful position in the local church. They either lead people toward God or they lead them astray. Teachers literally hold the souls of their students in their own hands. What an awesome responsibility! What an incomparable privilege!

This principle is put another way in Hebrews 13:17: "Obey your leaders and submit to their authority. They keep watch over you as men who must give an account." This applies to the highest level of leadership: To the elders of the church and to the pastor of the church. The top leaders of any church have a fearsome obligation: *To someday answer for the souls of those under their care.* They are even above the teachers in their obligation to God and to the congregation.

It is against this background that the words of Proverbs 31:2–5 come into focus. Any man wishing to be king must discipline himself. He must set aside any thoughts of sexual promiscuity and resist any temptation to dabble in alcohol. In the former case, promiscuity leads to moral and spiritual ruin; in the latter, alcohol may cloud the leader's judgment and cause him to make decisions that hurt others.

To whom much is given, much is required. Leaders have great privileges, but they pay a higher price. Many eyes are watching you. Don't let them down.

Lord Jesus, help me to remember that others are watching me all the time, and help me to live in the light of that knowledge. Amen.

Think of the people who look to you every day. Who are they? What are their names? Why are they looking to you? How does that make you feel? What do you think you owe them? If these verses were written to you personally, what other warnings would they include?

LOVE

✦

The Glue That Holds Life Together

Better a meal of vegetables where there is love than a fattened calf with hatred.

Proverbs 15:17

Several years ago I helped officiate at a wedding where the main ceremony was conducted by an older minister. He began his comments by saying that his wife had recently baked a loaf of zucchini bread. As he went on to extol his wife's virtues as a cook, I saw a few people in the audience smiling at each other. It didn't sound much like the normal wedding homily. But evidently the bread didn't turn out too well. He said it came out hard as a rock. I think his exact words were, "It was like a brick." By this time we were all laughing, and I think a few people wondered if he had lost his mind. Upon investigation, he and his wife soon discovered the problem. She had forgotten the baking powder, causing the bread not to rise, turning it into something more or less like a brick, and definitely inedible. The point, said the old gentleman, was clear. Without baking powder, zucchini bread won't turn out right. In the same way, love is the baking powder of marriage. With it, you can build a marriage that will be warm and delightful. Without it, the marriage is "like a brick."

I think my pastor friend was on to something. Love is the key, especially for the husband. If he leaves it out, nothing else he puts in will make any difference. If he puts love in, he can forget a lot of other ingredients and still have a happy marriage.

I saw this illustrated at the funeral of a dear friend. She and her husband loved each other deeply and had enjoyed nearly thirty good years together. Just before they closed the casket for the last time, her husband kissed her forehead and then knelt in prayer. As they took the casket away for burial, he reached out with his hand, patted it as it rolled by, and said, "I loved you so much. I loved you so much."

The soloist at the funeral overheard him say those words. As soon as the service was over, he called his wife, told her what had happened, and said, "Sweetheart, don't let me ever take you for granted."

That's a lesson we all need to learn. What we have is not ours to keep. The blessings we enjoy today will someday be taken from us. Nothing in this life lasts forever. Life is too short to take your blessings for granted. Make sure that the people you love know it.

The lesson of this proverb is clear. It is better to have love in the home than a large income or three cars in the garage. Better to eat boiled potatoes with those you love than filet mignon with people you can't stand. This is not an argument against wealth, but it is a reminder that money can't buy everything. If you don't have love, you are poor indeed.

Lord, help me to appreciate what I have while it is still mine to enjoy. Amen.

Are you taking your loved ones for granted? Before you say yes or no, consider how they might answer that question.

Who really needs to hear you say, "I love you"? Before you read another word, put this book down and tell them yourself.

MARRIAGE

❖

A Gift from God

He who finds a wife finds what is good and receives favor from the Lord.

Proverbs 18:22

An old preacher used to introduce his marriage ceremony with these words: "John, matrimony is a blessing to few, a curse to many, and an uncertainty to us all. John, will you venture?"

It is natural to want to venture. *The impulse to spend to your life with another person is put in the human heart by God Himself.* It is part of His original plan for the human race. Mankind did not begin as a unit, but as a united pair. We were born in wedlock.

It is no exaggeration to say that we were made for marriage. When all is said and done, and when the final count is taken, most people will be married at some time or another. Not that marriage is better than singleness. It all depends on the two people who are married and the one person who is single. Many people can best fulfill God's will for their lives by remaining single forever (1 Corinthians 7:7–8). Others may choose to marry later in life. But that should not obscure the main point: Marriage is one of God's best gifts to the human race because it establishes a relationship that is more intimate than any other human experience. You become "one flesh," which contains the idea of being glued together face-to-face. In marriage two separate people become truly one. They think as one, they act as one, they speak as one. Two people uniquely created by God—but in the act of marriage they become one flesh, proving that in God's arithmetic, one plus one still equals one.

That leads to an important truth found in Ephesians 5:22–33: *A marriage between two Christians is meant by God to point to the relationship between Christ and the church.* The one leads to the other. The husband points to Christ and the wife points to the church. He provides an example of loving sacrifice and she provides an example of gracious submission. He leads, she follows. He loves, she responds. In a sense, *marriage is a God-ordained mirror in which we can view eternity.*

We are like actors on a stage, with the whole world watching. Our marriage is our starring role. When a husband plays his part well, when a wife plays her part well, the audience sees something deeper; they see Christ and the church. That's the way God set it up, which is why a Christian marriage either draws people to Christ or drives them further away.

I've got news for you. You are a missionary to that office—and your marriage is your message. You don't have to preach a sermon. *Your lifetime commitment to your husband or wife is a visible sermon that people see every day.*

How can you show God's love to others? Let them see it in your marriage. It's more effective than a hundred tracts or two hundred Scripture verses. *People may doubt the things you say, but they cannot deny the reality of a truly Christian marriage.*

Lord God, may my marriage be a window in time through which others may catch a glimpse of eternity. Amen.

What kind of marriage did your parents have? If you are married, how is your relationship similar and how is it different? If you are single, would you want your marriage to be like the one your parents had?

If you are married, take a moment to pray for your mate right now.

MERCY

---❖---

Doing unto Others
As God Has Done unto You

A kind man benefits himself.

Proverbs 11:17a

Whoever is kind to the needy honors God.

Proverbs 14:31b

He who is kind to the poor lends to the Lord, and he will reward him for what he has done.

Proverbs 19:17

The principal Hebrew word for mercy is *racham*, which speaks of an emotional response to the needs of others. It means to feel the pain of another person so deeply that you are compelled to do something about it. *The ancients believed that the seat of the emotions was found in the intestinal area.* That is why the King James Version uses the phrase "bowels of mercy." When we say, "I have a gut feeling" about something, we are using the same concept.

   Mercy is an attribute of God's character. First Chronicles 21:13 tells us that "his mercy is very great." Nehemiah 9:31 speaks of "your great mercy." Luke 1:78 tells us that Christ came because of the "tender mercy" of our God. Romans 9:16 says that God's election springs

John 3:16

from His mercy. Ephesians 2:4 says that God is "rich in mercy." And Hebrews 4:16 tells us that when we come to Jesus in prayer we are coming to a throne of grace where we can receive mercy and find grace. According to Titus 3:5, God saved us because of his mercy. James 5:11 declares that "the Lord is full of compassion and mercy."

> The quality of mercy is not strained;
> It droppeth as the gentle rain from heaven.

These famous lines from William Shakespeare's *Merchant of Venice* are true in every way. *Mercy always comes down.* It starts with God and moves to man; it begins in heaven and ends on earth. You don't bargain for mercy, for to make a bargain you've got to have something to offer—and we have nothing to offer God. And mercy is indeed like the gentle rain that softens the hard soil of the human heart.

We need this because we are sinners worse than we know. *Even the best Christian would have no hope of heaven without the shining mercy of God.* If God did not forgive and keep on forgiving, if He did not continue to pour out His mercy like the "gentle rain from heaven," we would be utterly and completely lost.

Here's a simple definition of mercy: *Doing unto others as God has done unto you.* How has God treated you? Has God blessed you? Then bless others. Has God forgiven you? Then forgive others. Has God lifted you up when you were down? Then lift others up when they are down.

Has God overlooked your faults? Then overlook the faults of others. *The ABC's of wisdom says?*

Mercy includes three elements:

1. "I see the need"—that's *recognition*.
2. "I am moved by the need"—that's *motivation*.
3. "I move to meet the need"—that's *action*.

Make me a Blessing

Mercy is one of God's chief attributes. It is a fundamental part of His basic nature. *When I show mercy, I am in the place of God in someone's life*. I am doing to them what God would do. The world cannot see mercy in the abstract but only in the concrete. If you and I don't show mercy, where in the world will it be found?

> *Holy Father, as You have shown mercy to me, now enable me to show mercy to others. Amen.*

How has God blessed you in the last year? How could you be a greater blessing to others?

Think of a time when someone showed mercy to you. Think of a time when you showed mercy to someone else. In retrospect, which time was more personally satisfying to you?

MODERATION

❋

A Happy Middle-Class Life

Two things I ask of you, O Lord; do not refuse me before I die: Keep falsehood and lies far from me; give me neither poverty nor riches, but give me only my daily bread. Otherwise, I may have too much and disown you and say, "Who is the Lord?" Or I may become poor and steal, and so dishonor the name of my God.

Proverbs 30: 7–9

This is a prayer by a man who has seen too much. With his own eyes he has seen men lie and cheat to get to the top, only to be toppled by their own dishonesty. So he asks to be kept from the slightest hint of falsehood. He has also watched poor men steal in their desperation and he has seen the rich say, "God? If there is a God, I don't need Him." So he asks instead for what we might call a happy, middle-class life: "Give me only my daily bread."

This recalls the famous fourth petition of the Lord's Prayer: "Give us this day our daily bread." Bread in Scripture is more than just literal bread; it's also a symbol for all the physical and material needs of life. The Small Catechism by Martin Luther contains a section on the Lord's Prayer. This is what he says about "Give us today our daily bread":

What does this mean? God gives daily bread indeed without our prayer, and also to all the wicked. But we pray in this petition that he would lead us to know it and to receive our daily bread with thanksgiving.

What is meant by daily bread? Everything that belongs to the support and wants of the body, such as food, drink, clothing, shoes, house, home, field, cattle, money, goods, a pious spouse, pious children, pious servants, pious and faithful rulers, good government, good weather, peace, health, discipline, honor, good friends, faithful neighbors, and the like.

"And the like" means anything he leaves out of the list. Which means that everything physical or material is contained in the expression *bread*. You are not just praying for physical bread; you are praying for all the physical and material needs of life.

By praying this way we learn the importance of moment-by-moment, 100 percent dependence upon God for the things that we need. By praying for something as humble as a loaf of bread we are learning that God cares about the tiniest details of life. As Matthew Henry says, this really means that the followers of Jesus Christ are to have "a hand to mouth existence."

We should pray for godly character and to be preserved from any circumstance that would keep us from achieving that character—whether poverty or riches. Since we don't know which would be to our ultimate advantage, a happy, middle-class life will be about right for most of us.

Heavenly Father, I'm trusting You to know what I really need. Please help me to be delighted with the decisions You make. Amen.

What two things would you like to ask from the Lord before you die? Could you sincerely pray this man's prayer from your heart?

What specific aspect of Christian character would you most like to develop in your own life over the next three months?

MOTIVES

❖

It's the Thought That Counts

All a man's ways seem right to him, but the Lord weighs the heart.

Proverbs 21:2

The man's case was very simple. That he had been cheated out of his job was clear enough. That he had also lost his temper once or twice was also very clear. His boss had it in for him and was probably looking for a way to get rid of him. Eventually he found it. It wasn't fair, but that's the way the cookie crumbles.

As he told me his story, I could sense his anger, his outrage, his frustration. The trouble didn't end when he lost his job. Now the company was fighting his unemployment claim. What about your union? He shrugged his shoulders and said they were doing what they could.

The real pain was not from the loss of a job, as terrible as that was. The real pain came from the anger eating away at his soul. The acid of resentment bubbled away like hot lava inside a volcano. "Pastor, the reason I came to see you was because I hate living like this. For the first time in my life I feel prejudice toward people whose skin doesn't happen to be white like mine. That's what's killing me. I can't stand it anymore."

When the woman told her side of the story, I could

feel the deep emotion in her words. "I'm not going to play the game any longer. For years people looked at me and said, 'Everything is all right. She's got the perfect life.' But it's not all right. It's hasn't been right for years."

Now at last, after suffering in silence for too long, she has decided to get better. That's a risky step because some of her friends won't understand her decision. Sometimes people feel better if you just "grin and bear it" and pretend that life is rosy. That way no one has to worry about messy things like coming to grips with your past. Nice people play the game, even if things aren't really so nice behind closed doors.

My friend said something that stuck in my mind. "Do you remember the story of Saul on the road to Damascus? It hit me just like that. I can't explain it other than to say that in one blinding moment of truth I saw myself. Since that moment everything has changed. There's so much pain now that I feel overwhelmed. But I know that going through pain is the only way to grow."

She's right. Real growth only comes through pain. My friend who lost his job is learning that truth. So is my friend who decided not to play the game anymore.

Do you want to get better? You can, but you've got to go through pain to get there. To paraphrase the words of Jesus, the truth will set you free, but it will hurt you first. Or, to paraphrase Solomon, you may think you're OK the way you are, but that's not what matters. God starts with the heart and works from there. He searches and sifts and weighs your motives. Nothing escapes His piercing glance. This is frightening at first, but then the healing begins.

Search me, O God, and try my heart. See if there be any wicked way in me. Let the truth come out, even if it hurts. Amen.

How would you feel if the thoughts of your heart were revealed for everyone to see? What part of your heart would you like the Lord to search, sift, and heal right now?

NOBILITY

※

The Legacy of a Godly Wife

A wife of noble character who can find? She is worth far more than rubies.

Proverbs 31:10

The final section of Proverbs is an acrostic, a poem in which each verse begins with a different letter of the Hebrew alphabet. One commentator calls this "an alphabet of wifely excellence." The phrase *of noble character* translates a very common word (used 246 times in the Old Testament) that in various passages refers to strength, courage, valor, ingenuity, and wealth. Perhaps the last meaning was on the author's mind when he wrote that a godly wife is worth "more than rubies." Just as a good name is more desirable than great riches (Proverbs 22:1), so also is a wife of noble character a greater treasure than the riches of the world.

This wife has many admirable traits. She is trustworthy (v. 11), a blessing and not a burden (v. 12), fully committed to her husband (v. 12), hardworking (v. 13), industrious (vv. 13-15), well organized (v. 15), shrewd in business (v. 16), confident (v. 18), diligent (v. 18), a self-starter (v. 19), compassionate (v. 20), prepared for future contingencies (v. 21), well dressed (v. 22), a strong boost to her husband's career (v. 23), active as a businesswoman in her community (v. 24), a woman of honor (v. 25), both wise and kind (v. 26), and a homemaker in the best sense of the word (v. 27). As a result, her children and her husband praise her (vv. 28–29) because she does not depend on charm or beauty but instead fears the Lord (v. 30). Her fame spreads throughout the city and she enjoys the reward she has earned (v. 31).

Throughout the centuries, women have marveled at this depiction of the ideal wife. She is a wife, a mother, and a very successful businesswoman. If on first reading this seems more like Superwoman than a real woman, it may be that the author is describing not one particular woman, but the life of any godly woman who supports her husband, loves her children, takes care of her family, and uses her gifts and talents to bless others.

She is the kind of wife a woman should be and the kind of woman a man should choose to marry. Although we are not told who she was, we know what she was—a woman who feared the Lord and put her faith into practice. That is the key. Because she reverenced God, everything else in her life stayed in balance. Because she loved her husband, she supported him and used her gifts to increase the family's resources. As she found her fulfillment in the mundane tasks of life, God blessed the entire family and gave her honor throughout the whole community.

It is no accident that Proverbs closes with this lengthy portrait. The wife of noble character stands in sharp contrast to the contentious woman (19:13) and the immoral woman (chaps. 5–7). In the end those who know her best give her the praise she deserves. In her husband's eyes, there is no other woman like her. Her children call her blessed. Everyone who knows her praises her.

Here is a worthy model for every wife and for every woman who hopes to be married one day. Study this passage; learn these principles; ask God to make you a woman of noble character. The praise she received is also meant for you.

Lord God, may I be worthy of praise by those who know me best and love me most. Amen.

Which attributes of this noble woman most impress you? How does your life stack up against hers? How would your friends answer that question? Which of her qualities would you most like to develop over the next few months?

OBEDIENCE

---※---

The Benefits of Playing by the Rules

Now then, my sons, listen to me; blessed are those who keep my ways.

Proverbs 8:32

Here is a simple promise from God. Those who walk in the way of wisdom will be blessed. The word *listen* means to hear *and* to obey. After all, any fool can hear the truth, but the truth means nothing until it has penetrated the heart and changed the way you live. A thousand sermons on purity won't keep you from a tragic mistake until you set your heart to obey God's command.

A friend pressed a cartoon into my hand just before a worship service. Because it was a long day and I was busy, I didn't get a chance to look at it until Monday. The cartoon strip is called "Hagar the Horrible." It shows a short, squatly Viking laboring up a steep, snow-covered mountain. As he nears the top, he cries out, "What is the key to happiness?" The wise man answers, "Abstinence, poverty, fasting and celibacy." With a crestfallen look, the Viking shouts, "Is there anyone else up there I could talk to?"

Good question. All of us would like it if there were someone else "up there" who would tell us what we really want to hear—that life is basically easy, that the key to happiness is self-indulgence, that you can take shortcuts and still make it to the top.

As I ponder the matter, the following facts seem true to me:

1. Life is hard.
2. Even the best days are filled with difficulty.
3. We're all secretly looking for "someone else" to tell us what we want to hear.
4. Abstinence, poverty, fasting, and celibacy are not much fun—but they bring more lasting joy than their opposites.
5. Happiness isn't found in self-indulgence.
6. In general, happiness isn't "found" at all.
7. Happiness comes as a by-product of other things.
8. There is little, if any, correlation between leisure, luxury, and happiness.
9. Obedience won't necessarily make you happy, but disobedience will definitely disappoint you in the end.

On the campus of the Moody Bible Institute there is a small plaque on the brick wall of one of the dormitories. This is what it says: "Near this spot in the spring of 1889 Dwight L. Moody knelt in prayer and asked God for this land on which to build a Bible school." Underneath are the words of 1 John 2:17 from the King James Version: "He that doeth the will of God abideth forever."

Was D. L. Moody a happy man? Historians tell us

that he was a jovial, gregarious man whose heart burned with a passion to win the lost to Jesus Christ. His life stands as a testimony that the happiest people on earth are those who seek and find the will of God. If you seek happiness, you will never find it; if you seek to do the will of God, you will find more happiness by accident than most people find on purpose.

Lord God, I want to do Your will more than anything else. If that is not true of me, do whatever it takes to make it true. Amen.

Do you agree that happiness is a by-product of doing the will of God? How does your life match up with that principle? What act of obedience have you been putting off? What are you going to do about it?

OPEN-MINDEDNESS

—✦—

Take Time to Hear Both Sides

The first to present his case seems right, till another comes forward and questions him.

Proverbs 18:17

Here is a piece of wisdom that could have been coined by Ben Franklin. There are two sides to every story—at least two and maybe more. This is the third warning in Proverbs 18 about the danger of forming hasty opinions. Verse 2 says that "a fool finds no pleasure in understanding but delights in airing his own opinions." Verse 13 adds that "he who answers before listening—that is his folly and his shame." Taken together, these three verses remind us that, in order to find the truth, we must first stop talking (v. 2), start listening (v. 13), and make sure we hear both sides before making up our minds (v. 17).

"The first to present his case seems right." Certainly we all feel this way about ourselves. We all learn to make excuses early on—the dog ate our homework, we "accidentally" told a lie, we meant to return the phone call but then we forgot. If we are in a dispute with a friend or a coworker, we naturally bend the facts in our own direction, subtly shading the truth to make our case look stronger than it really is. We are not intentionally lying, which would unquestionably be sinful. No, what we are doing is harder to detect, though no less wrong. We are presenting the facts to make ourselves appear in the most favorable light possible. Most of us do this so instinctively that we don't even realize it. We are all by nature biased in our own favor.

"Till another comes forward and questions him." Suddenly our explanation doesn't seem so strong and our excuses look like . . . excuses. What seemed to be an adequate defense now seems small and selfish and perhaps even deceitful.

For most of us, there is huge room for improvement in this area, both in how we present ourselves and how we evaluate others. On the one hand, we ought to tell "the truth, the whole truth, and nothing but the truth" about our own words and deeds. If we would do that, no surprise witness could ever impeach us. On the other hand, this proverb urges us to be slow to evaluate the facts of a given case. Here is a word of warning for teachers, principals, bosses, managers, department heads, and all those in authority. Don't be taken in by the first person you hear. Take time to hear both sides. Ask hard questions. Make sure you get the facts.

Better to delay a decision than to wish you had. Better to be thought too cautious than to be, in fact, too hasty.

It was said of Christ that He was a man without guile. That means He had nothing hidden because He had nothing to hide. He never exaggerated because He was Truth personified. He never tried to fool anyone, and He was never fooled by anyone. That's the standard for us to follow.

> *Lord Jesus, help me have the grace to tell the truth and wisdom to discern the truth today. Amen.*

Do you agree that by nature we all shade the truth in our own favor? Name an area of your life where you need to stop making excuses and start telling the truth.

Can you think of a situation facing you right now where you need wisdom to determine the true facts of the case?

OVERINDULGENCE

---❖---

Too Much of a Good Thing

If you find honey, eat just enough—too much of it, and you will vomit.

Proverbs 25:16

Perhaps this doesn't seem like a life-changing issue, and it might not be—until you begin to vomit. You don't realize the problem until it has overwhelmed you. As Derek Kidner has remarked, there is a fundamental difference between a healthy appetite and greed.

In some ways this desire to always have more goes all the way back to the Garden of Eden, where God offered Adam and Eve their choice of the fruit set before them. "Look in any direction," God seemed to say. "Do you like peaches? Nectarines? Pears? Plums? Grapes? Would you like a fresh orange or possibly a nice fruit salad for lunch? Whatever you see, you can have. It all belongs to you."

There was only one restriction. "Don't touch the tree of the knowledge of good and evil." Thousands of trees were theirs for the taking. All the fruit they could ever want and more besides. They were in paradise and God offered them enormous freedom. "Pick your fruit and eat to your heart's content. Just don't touch that one tree. Everything else is yours for the taking."

Not surprisingly, that's exactly where the serpent attacked (Genesis 3:1–6). He questioned God's goodness and implied that God was holding out on them. "He doesn't want you to be happy and fulfilled. He's keeping the best for Himself. He was lying when He said you would die."

Someone was indeed lying, and he hasn't stopped lying since. The serpent still whispers in our ear that we'll be happy if only we spend more, buy more, move up to a larger home, take a new job, move to a new city, get on the fast track, loosen up our rigid standards, learn to move with the movers and shake with the shakers.

His greatest feat may be in convincing unhappy spouses that the grass is greener on the other side of the fence. So husbands have affairs and wives file for divorce—or vice versa. At its heart, the current divorce craze is driven by the belief that human happiness and God's will must be identical. "How can God be pleased with a marriage where we are so miserable together?" Will the God who said "I hate divorce" (Malachi 2:16) be more pleased when you are no longer married?

Ever since Eden, men and women have sought to find happiness by pushing beyond the limits established by God. Deep down we doubt God's goodness and we think that if a little is good, a lot must be better. So we overeat, overspend, and overindulge all our appetites. If it feels good, we do it, even if God has said it is wrong. Something in us makes us push the limits, hoping to find happiness. Or peace. Or satisfaction. Or joy.

When will we learn that there is no fulfillment outside of God? His ways are always best. When we break the rules, we pay the price of a seriously upset stomach.

Lord God, save me from the folly of thinking that I need something besides You to be truly happy today. Amen.

In what areas of your life are you tempted to overindulge? When does it happen most often? What one thing would make you happy right now?

What does it mean to you to be satisfied with Jesus?

PARENTS

❖

Treat Them with Respect

My son, keep your father's commands and do not forsake your mother's teaching.

Proverbs 6:20

The eye that mocks a father, that scorns obedience to a mother, will be pecked out by the ravens of the valley, will be eaten by the vultures.

Proverbs 30:17

The fifth commandment says, "Honor your father and your mother" (Exodus 20:12). For too long we have relegated this commandment to young children and sometimes even used it as a club over their heads. *But God never intended that this commandment be aimed primarily at young children.* This commandment is primarily for grown-up children. It is God's way of telling us how to treat our parents!

But how can we honor our parents when we no longer live under their authority? *First, by speaking well of them.* Sometimes I hear adults saying terribly disrespectful things about their parents. They speak with bitterness and anger over things that happened many years ago. That raises a question: *How do you speak well of people who hurt you deeply?* Here I think we're left with some advice we all learned as children. "If you can't say something nice, say nothing at all." Speak well of your parents if you can; if you can't, refuse to speak evil of them.

Second, by obeying them. This sounds odd to our modern way of thinking. For many people the whole point of moving away from home is so that you won't have to obey your parents anymore. Most of us have heard it said that while you don't have to obey your parents, you always have to honor them. That's true enough, but it doesn't grasp the full biblical implication of the fifth commandment. In God's eyes we are forever children, always under obligation to honor and—as far as possible—to obey our parents.

Third, we honor our parents by forgiving them. Here we come to the heart of the problem for many people. How do you honor parents who have hurt and abused you? By choosing to forgive the unforgivable. *We must not use the hurts of the past as an excuse to evade this commandment.* Think of it this way: If we do not forgive our parents, we may repeat their mistakes with our own children.

Fourth, by not forsaking them. At this point we have the example of Jesus who, while hanging on the cross, took time to remember His aging mother. To His mother He said, "Dear woman, here is your son." To John He said, "Here is your mother" (*see* John 19:26–27). While dying for the sins of the world, He took time to keep the fifth commandment!

D. L. Moody said, "I have lived over sixty years, and I have learned one thing if I have learned nothing else—no man or woman who dishonors his father or mother ever prospers."

This commandment is the one that helps you obey all the rest. *The first place you can show the reality of your religion is at home.* To say it another way, religion that doesn't begin at home doesn't begin at all.

> *Lord God, if I would call You heavenly Father, I must learn to honor my earthly father and mother. Show me what that means. Amen.*

Do you find it easy to honor your parents? Why or why not?

Which of the four steps listed above is most difficult for you? Name one way you could honor your parents today.

PASSION

---❖---

The Flame That Keeps a Marriage Burning

A loving doe, a graceful deer—may her breasts satisfy you always, may you ever be captivated by her love.

Proverbs 5:19

There are many secrets to a good marriage, such as respect, communication, commitment, forgiveness, a good sense of humor, and the ability to disagree agreeably. While it may not be the most important factor, certainly a healthy sexual relationship must be high on any such list.

Solomon emphasizes this truth in his warning against adultery in Proverbs 5. First, he details the terrible cost of unfaithfulness. You lose your strength (v. 9), your wealth (v. 10), your health (v. 11), and your reputation (v. 14). Is there any good news? Yes. Proverbs 5:15–18 says,

> Drink water from your own cistern, running water from your own well. Should your springs overflow in the streets, your streams of water in the public squares? Let them be yours alone, never to be shared with strangers. May your fountain be blessed, and may you rejoice in the wife of your youth.

God has given you a biblical way for handling the sexual drive within you. It's called marriage. Verse 19 offers a graphic explanation: "A loving doe, a graceful deer—may her breasts satisfy you always, may you ever be captivated [in the Hebrew this word means "intoxicated"] by her love." Verse 20 gives the alternative, "Why be captivated, my son, by an adulteress? Why embrace the bosom of another man's wife?" God has created a way that is better than looking at dirty movies. He has created a way that is better than going to some prostitute, a way that is better than looking at some cheap magazine, than flirting with someone else on the job. It's called loving your wife. If you love your wife and enjoy her and her body, you will find release for what God has put within you. As man and woman come from the hand of almighty God, they come as male and female. Within that relationship, the sexual relationship of a man and woman is holy, righteous, pure, good, and ought to be enjoyed. That's what the Bible says. To men who feel this tremendous sexual urge, don't go running somewhere else; go back to the wife God has given you.

There you have the whole case for marital faithfulness. Stay home and enjoy your wife. Don't be a fool and look at some other woman. Enjoy the wife you have. Let her body satisfy you. Be intoxicated with her love.

If you wonder about the propriety of that statement, I encourage you to read the Song of Solomon. It contains the Bible's most detailed description of romantic love between a man and a woman. It is sensual, yet pure; frank, yet chaste; erotic, yet ennobling. Many couples would find their love life rejuvenated simply by reading the Song of Solomon out loud together. So how does a wife keep her husband satisfied? God has given you a way. Men, how do you stay satisfied? Solomon—who had great experience in this area—spelled it out. Enjoy your wife. And not just her cooking either.

Father, I thank You for creating the human race as male and female. When I am tempted to misuse Your gifts, remind me of the joy that comes from following Your plan. Amen.

If you are single, will you commit yourself to sexual purity in all your relationships?

If you are married, will you commit yourself to faithfulness so that you can enjoy your spouse as God intended?

PATIENCE

The Waiting Game

Better a patient man than a warrior, a man who controls his temper than one who takes a city.

Proverbs 16:32

Regarding this verse, John Phillips points out the difference between Joab and David. As David's chief general, Joab knew how to take a city. In many ways he was the General Patton of the Old Testament. He knew how to fight and he knew how to win. He wasn't afraid to attack, even if the odds were stacked against him. After all, he earned his spurs (so to speak) by taking the Jebusite fortress, which not even Joshua could conquer. He did it by climbing up the rock-hewn passage from which the Jebusites drew their water supply (see 2 Samuel 5:6–8). Joab knew how to take a city.

But in every way David was a greater man. When provoked by Saul again and again, he refused to retaliate. When he had a chance to kill Saul in the cave near En Gedi (1 Samuel 24), he refused, saying he could not touch the Lord's anointed. He proclaimed his own innocence and then declared, "May the Lord judge between you and me. And may the Lord avenge the wrongs you have done to me, but my hand will not touch you" (v. 12).

There are two interesting facts here: The first is that David was not shy about pointing out the truth. He plainly said that Saul had wronged him. Sometimes in our hurry to reconcile we overlook the fact that wrong has been done. It's rarely true that "we're both right and we're both wrong." That implies a kind of neutrality that cancels the need to make moral judgments. Such a position is useful only for those who live in a fantasy world. Saul was wrong. David knew he was wrong—and he plainly said so.

There is a second helpful fact here. David understood something many of us never grasp. When it comes to revenge, God is much better at it than we are. That's because He looks down from heaven and sees all sides of every issue. He knows who is right and He knows who is wrong. So often our perspective is clouded and our judgment faulty. We see our side and only our side. But God knows. And He will not forget to avenge the wrongs done to His children.

David understood that God was ready, willing, and able to take care of him. And whenever God got ready, Saul would be out of the way and David would ascend to the throne. If God wanted Saul removed, there were ten thousand ways He could do it. God didn't need David's help. Even when David was clearly the better man, even when Saul had gone nuts, even when God had rejected Saul, He still didn't need David's help.

How many sins are committed because we are in a hurry, because under pressure we give in to our passions, because in the crunch we cut corners we would never cut otherwise. How many stupid decisions we make because we aren't willing to wait for God.

I take great personal comfort in this—that God is not so unjust as to forget His children. And when we suffer for doing what is right, God sees and He remembers. That's a promise you can take to the bank.

Lord God, when I am tempted to take matters into my own hands, remind me to wait lest by my impatience I spoil Your work on my behalf. Amen.

Someone has called waiting the hardest discipline of the Christian life. Do you agree?

In what areas of your life are you currently waiting for God to work? Why is it especially important to wait for God when our friends turn against us?

PATRIOTISM

❖

Fear the Lord *and* the King

Fear the Lord and the king, my son, and do not join with the rebellious.

Proverbs 24:21

I t is often said that God only established three institutions—the home, the church, and the state. In so doing, He gave us explicit instructions on how all three were to operate. Most Christians know a great deal about what God has to say about the home and church. *We know much less about what God says about the state and how we should relate to it.* For instance, what does it mean to be a Christian living under a pagan government? Is violent revolution ever justified? Is it wrong to pay taxes to an unjust government? What about picketing abortion clinics? Under what circumstances should Christians disobey the law? What about the separation of church and state? Should Christians serve in the armed forces? How do you respond when those over you are corrupt?

These are all important questions, and none of them admits to a simple answer. Romans 13:1 tells us that "everyone must submit himself to the governing authorities, for there is no authority except that which God has established. The authorities that exist have been established by God." The word *authority* is very broad. It means "right" or "privilege." *An authority is anyone who has the right to do something.* If your job gives you the right to make certain decisions, when you are on the job, you are an "authority." *Seen in another light, an authority is anyone who has the right to make decisions that directly affect your life.*

Then there is an explicit directive. "Submit to the governing authorities." No ifs, ands, or buts. Just the word *submit.* Let me a share a simple definition that may help you. *Submission is believing that God is able to accomplish His will in my life through the people He has placed in authority over me.* That's a crucial definition because it focuses the attention on God, not on the person over you. We all have to contend at times with unsaved husbands, mean-spirited parents, cranky bosses, and teachers who can't wait for the end of the semester. Sometimes we'll work for people we can't stand. Or live with people who treat us cruelly. Or suffer under a government that consistently promotes evil.

What do you do, then? Actually, you have many options. *The most important thing is the attitude of your heart.* You must submit to the one in authority, in the sense that you must believe God has put that person in your life for a purpose and that God's will is somehow being done through that person, even if you don't see it and don't understand it.

This, by the way, is the basis for treating our leaders with respect. *Christians ought to lead the way in showing honor to human authorities because we understand they are appointed by God.* Whom God has appointed, I must not treat lightly.

If we believe what the Bible says, it will make us better Christians and ultimately better citizens. We may disagree, but we won't resort to violence and we won't join the ranks of the rebellious.

> *Heavenly Father, since I am a citizen of two realms, help me to represent You well by showing proper honor to those in authority over me. Amen.*

In what areas of life are you in authority and in what areas are you under authority? What does it mean for you to show honor to those who are over you? When is it a struggle for you?

PEACEMAKING

✦

The Mark of the Children of God

There is deceit in the hearts of those who plot evil, but joy for those who promote peace.

Proverbs 12:20

A few years ago pollster George Gallup surveyed Americans on the top five questions they would most like to ask God. The list included the following question: "Will there ever be lasting world peace?"

It's a fitting question to ask as we near the end of the bloodiest century in world history. *More people have died in this century because of warfare than in any other since the dawn of the human race.* As President Eisenhower once said, we have become a race of intellectual giants and moral pygmies. Despite our great technological advances, we continue to devise more efficient means of killing each other.

In this bloody world, peace must be made. Peace never happens by chance. Someone has to drag the combatants to the table and give them a reason to put down their arms. Jesus never said, "Blessed are the peace*wishers* or the peace*hopers* or the peace*dreamers*." But He did say, "Blessed are the peace*makers*" (Matthew 5:9).

What is a peacemaker? Here's a working definition: *A peacemaker is someone who is actively working to reconcile men to God and to one another.* He (or she) is a "minister of reconciliation" who has been given the "message of reconciliation" (see 2 Corinthians 5:18–21).

Please note that peacemaking is a spiral that begins close to home. It starts in your closest and most intimate relationships—between husbands and wives, parents and children, brothers and sisters, uncles and aunts. Then it moves out to your extended family—your close friends at church, on the job, and in the classroom. Only then does peacemaking move out to more remote relationships—in the village, the city, the state, the nation, and the world.

Peacemaking is not an easy business. It is costly, time-consuming, painful, and emotionally exhausting. Those who do it will often be misunderstood.

Our problem tends to be at the level of motivation. *We know that peace is hard to make and even harder to keep.* It's usually easier to walk away from a problem. Why get involved in someone else's difficulty? Or we try and are rebuffed or even attacked and criticized for our efforts. So we tend to despair and give up even before we get started.

But everyone can do something.

- You've got a telephone. Make a call.
- You've got paper. Write a letter.
- You've got a kitchen. Make a meal.
- You've got a billfold. Give some money.
- You've got two hands. Put them to work for others.
- You've got two feet. Go see a friend in pain.

- You've got two ears. Listen to the cries of the wounded.
- You've got two eyes. Lift them up to see the world as God sees it.
- You've got two lips. Preach the gospel of peace.

There is so much war, so much strife, so much pain in the world. That means there is plenty of work for you to do. Every tiny step receives God's blessing.

How do you get involved in the world? Be a peacemaker!

What will you be called? A child of God!

Prince of Peace, make me an instrument of Your peace so that others will know that I am a child of God. Amen.

Why is peacemaking not a popular occupation? Name three situations where you could make a difference as a peacemaker. What hinders you from getting involved?

PERSEVERANCE

❖

The Lost Art of Stick-to-it-ivity

Four things on earth are small, yet they are extremely wise: Ants are creatures of little strength, yet they store up their food in the summer; coneys are creatures of little power, yet they make their home in the crags; locusts have no king, yet they advance together in ranks; a lizard can be caught with the hand, yet it is found in kings' palaces.

Proverbs 30:24–28

Ants . . . coneys . . . locusts . . . lizards. What do they have in common, and why did the wise man (named *Agur* in 30:1) group them together? For one thing, they are all small and often overlooked. Yet even the tiniest of God's creatures have big lessons to teach us. Ants prepare for the future, coneys survive in hostile environments, locusts fly in swarms, and lizards were caught and then placed in the palace to find and eat bugs and insects. Perhaps the central fact is simply that these creatures accomplish great feats without the benefit of any other earthly advantage save their own God-imparted wisdom. Despite their small size, they accomplish huge feats. They are small but smart.

Ants are singled out because they overcome their small size by working together to prepare for the future. No excuses here. Just teamwork in the hot summer days to lay up food for the cold winter to come. Coneys are rock-badgers who thrive among the rocks of the wilderness. Few animals dare to venture where the coneys call home. Most of us have seen pictures of huge swarms of locusts darkening the skies as they prepare to descend on a field to strip it bare. One locust could never do the job, but because they move "in ranks," there is nothing left when they are finished. Lizards may be harmless pets but they also serve the king's purpose. The lizard goes where others never enter—not even with bribes or force of arms.

Taken together, these four examples suggest several important lessons: *First, even the tiniest creatures have a purpose in God's plan.* Although we may not personally appreciate locusts or lizards, they have a purpose no less than we do. This is part of God's providence that extends to the tiniest details of life. *Second, since we all have limitations of one kind or another, success comes to those who discover what they can do, and then do it.* Some of us aren't even as "successful" as the ants and the lizards because we focus on what we can't do instead of what we can. *Third, just be yourself and you'll turn out all right.* Let the ants be ants; the lizards, lizards; the snakes, snakes; and the hippos, hippos. Can you imagine a huge hippopotamus trying to sneak unseen into a king's palace? It's not likely to work. But when you need a huge, lumbering animal to cavort in the water, you won't call a lizard either. A hippo is what you need.

Be yourself and do what God has called you to do.

Just keep on doing it day in and day out. That's what perseverance is all about.

Lord, give me the grace to keep on doing what You called me to do. And save me from the folly of making excuses for not doing my job today. Amen.

Name one positive character quality associated with ants, coneys, locusts, and lizards. Now rate yourself in each one of those qualities.

Where do you most need perseverance right now?

PERSPECTIVE

❖

No Milk Without Manure

*Where there are no oxen, the manger is empty, but from the
strength of an ox comes an abundant harvest.*

Proverbs 14:4

Every farmer understands this verse. If you want a
clean stable, get rid of the oxen. But if you want cattle, you've got to put up with noise, trouble, clutter, and
mess. Or as Dr. Ryrie succinctly puts it, "No milk without manure."

Wise parents know what this is about it. Raising children can be a messy business. I speak as the father of
three very active teenage sons. When people ask me what
it's like in our house, I usually reply with two words: "It's
loud." Boys make noise. They also take up lots of space,
eat lots of food, drape themselves over the chairs, camp
out in front of the TV, and turn the trash can into a bas-
ketball goal. Every night they call their friends or their
friends call them. When I ask how they are doing in
school, it's always, "Don't worry, Dad. We're doing fine."

Recently Nicholas, our youngest son, spent hours
putting together a model of a 1940 Ford Coupe. When
he finished, there were bits of plastic, torn decals, and
globs of glue spread across the basement floor. "Dad,
look at the engine," he said triumphantly. "It has fifteen

different parts"—which he proceeded to point out to me one by one. As I study the model two months later, it sits in a place of honor on his desk, next to his portable calculator and under his Chicago Bulls banner, not far from the cage containing Sir John of Camelot, his pet hamster. There are plastic newspaper bags on the floor, left over from his weekly paper route. As I survey the scene, it seems to me that his room is a little messy. Not terrible, but it could use some straightening up. When I tell him that, he grins, rolls his eyes, and says, "Oh, Dad"—in a tone that tells me that I just don't understand his world at all.

It's true, I don't. But I have learned to have some long-range perspective, to understand that raising children requires a mix of love, humor, patience, persistence, honesty, clear guidelines, and a healthy dose of prayer. Even then, we all know that boys and girls grow up into young adults with minds of their own.

If you want a perfectly clean house all the time, don't have children. That should solve the problem. But if you have children, don't be surprised by the noise, clatter, clutter, commotion, action, energy, laughter, and music that children bring with them. It is no accident that life begins with a slap on the bottom and a loud cry. That's a harbinger of things to come.

Children are a heritage from the Lord. They are also a handful from the Lord. Your manger will never be quite the same again. But years from now you will have no regrets when the Lord brings in the harvest.

Lord, when I am frazzled, help me to see beyond the moment to better things yet to come. Amen.

In what areas of your life do you need long-range perspective right now? Why is that perspective especially important when raising children?

If you have children, what kind of "harvest" are you praying for in their lives?

PRAISE

❖

Can You Handle It?

The crucible for silver and the furnace for gold, but man is tested by the praise he receives.

Proverbs 27:21

For every person who can handle success, there are a thousand who can handle failure. As bad as it hurts to be on the bottom, sometimes it hurts worse to be on top. Praise brings with it four unseen dangers: (1) It may cause us to believe we are better than we really are; (2) it may lead us to think we deserve what we have; (3) it may blind us to our own weaknesses; and (4) it may lead to a place where we no longer think we need the Lord.

Praise may cause us to end up in the crucible, a fiery furnace where our motives will be severely tested and all that is false in us completely exposed. At that moment it will be difficult to remember that gold and silver are purified by passing through the fire. Though that image is often applied to trials, it also applies to our victories.

The spiritual truth behind this proverb is not hard to spot. Satan often attacks us at the point of our strength, not the point of our weakness. Should this surprise us? After all, why should Satan attack only in the point of your self-perceived weakness? If you know you have a weakness, that's the very area you will guard most carefully. If you know you have a problem with anger or with laziness or with lust or with gluttony, will you not be on your guard lest you fall?

But it is not so with your strengths. You take those areas for granted. You say, "That's not a problem for me. I have other problems, but that area is not really a temptation at all."

Watch out! Put up the red flag! There is danger ahead. When a person takes *any* area of life for granted, that's the one area Satan is most likely to attack. Why? Because that's the one area where you aren't watching for his attack.

At this point we do well to remember the Jewish leaders who believed on Jesus but would not confess Him for fear of the Pharisees. "They loved praise from men more than praise from God" (John 12:43). Praise is wonderful to receive, but when we love it too much it can lead us away from God.

The praise of others should not be rejected when offered in sincerity. However, we are not to build our lives around it, either. Don't believe everything people say about you—the good or the bad. You're not as good as your friends think you are and you're not as bad as your enemies say you are. As with most things in life, the truth is somewhere in the middle.

When someone compliments you on a job well done, smile, say thank you, and give the glory to God. But don't let it go to your head. Learn this lesson well or you'll end up doing more "hot time" in the crucible.

Lord, give me the grace to appreciate the praise I receive and to give You glory for any good thing I accomplish, for without You I can do nothing. Amen.

List your personal strengths. How have you been praised or affirmed in any of those areas recently?

Take a moment to offer each of those areas to the Lord along with any praise you might receive now or in the future.

PRIDE

❖

The First Deadly Sin

Pride goes before destruction, a haughty spirit before a fall.
Proverbs 16:18

There are several difficulties in talking about pride, one of the most obvious being that it is hard to define but easy to spot. We all know a prideful person when we see one. But what exactly is pride? As you think about the definition, a second problem pops up. Pride is not altogether bad. There is, after all, justifiable pride in a job well done, in a well-kept garden, in a project completed, in the accomplishments of those you love. When we say "I'm proud of you" to our grandchildren, are we committing a sin?

The answer, of course, is no. But even to ask the question shows how tricky pride is. Proverbs 8:13 associates pride with arrogance while 13:10 tell us that pride breeds quarrels. Proverbs 21:24 adds that when a man is both proud and arrogant, "'Mocker' is his name." It also helps to remember that pride was the sin that caused Satan to fall from heaven (see Isaiah 14:12–15; 1 Timothy 3:6). Five times he said "I will," setting the pattern of self-exaltation for all who follow him.

But what is the particular lesson of Proverbs 16:18? It serves as a warning to anyone who rises to a position of leadership or prominence. The higher you rise, the greater the possibility of a shocking fall. In the last few years we have seen the same scenario played out as notable political and religious leaders have toppled from their high positions, their individual sins many, their root sin always the same—pride, which led to overconfidence, which caused them to be careless about the details of life, which eventually led to a serious breach of ethics, which caused them to fall hard and fast.

Acts 12 offers one of the most shocking examples of this pattern. When Herod Agrippa I sat on his throne delivering a message to his people, they shouted, "This is the voice of a god, not of a man" (v. 22). Evidently the thought pleased him, for he did not stop their idolatrous praise. Verse 23 tells the story with straightforward simplicity: "Immediately, because Herod did not give praise to God, an angel of the Lord struck him down, and he was eaten by worms and died." Think about that for a moment. Is there a worse way to die than to be eaten by worms?

We may take several important lessons from all this. First, you're not as hot as you think you are. When Louis XIV died, he decreed that a candle be lit by his coffin, showing that he was the light of France. A priest entered the room, blew out the candle, and declared, "Only God is great." There is no room for pride when you realize that every good thing you possess was given to you by God. Second, it helps to have a few good friends who can prick your balloon when you start getting too full of hot air.

Third, you can either humble yourself or be humbled by God. The first is infinitely preferable. Just ask a man named Herod.

> *Lord, when I am tempted to think that I am someone special, remind me that without You I wouldn't even be able to pray this prayer. Amen.*

What is the difference between pride in a job well done and the sinful pride God hates?

Name the friends who can prick your balloon when you are full of hot air.

PROGRESS

❖

Walking Toward the Light

The path of the righteous is like the first gleam of dawn,
shining ever brighter till the full light of day.

Proverbs 4:18

Here is a wonderful promise for the believer. God has ordained that as we walk in His ways, obedient to His will, our path will grow brighter and brighter. Theologians call this "progressive sanctification," which refers to the process whereby we are changed little by little, day by day into the likeness of Jesus Christ (*see* 2 Corinthians 3:18).

This is God's promise, but like most of His promises, it isn't fulfilled all at once. No matter how long we live, God has more light for us to receive. We'll never be completely in "the light" until we stand in the presence of Jesus, the Light of the world.

Not long ago I ran into a friend who is involved in a twelve-step program. As we talked, he passed along a slogan that he first learned in his weekly meetings: "Our goal is not perfection, but progress."

A little bell started ringing in my mind when I heard those words. "Not perfection, but progress." My friend told me that whenever he falls back into his old way of thinking, he feels so defeated he wants to give up. When that happens, he said, the key is to remember that his goal is not perfection—which is always unattainable—but simple day-by-day progress.

What difference does it make?

- *Perfection says*, "I must do this right all the time or I am a failure." *Progress says*, "I know I'm going to fail occasionally, but that won't stop me from getting up and trying again."
- *Perfection says*, "If I fail, people will think I'm a loser." *Progress says*, "If I fail, people will understand as long as I don't give up and quit."
- *Perfection says*, "It's wrong to admit my weaknesses." *Progress says*, "Admitting my weaknesses is the only way to get better."
- *Perfection says*, "I've got all the answers." *Progress says*, "I've got a few answers and a lot of questions."
- *Perfection says*, "It's not my fault." *Progress says*, "I was wrong."
- *Perfection says*, "I can do it by myself." *Progress says*, "I think I can do it, but I need the help of God and a few good friends."

If we dwell on our failures, we will soon grow despondent. Who among us has not made mistakes that today make us blush with shame? But the past is more than a record of personal failure. It's also the story of God's amazing grace to us. Time after time God bailed us out when by all rights He should have given up on us. We were bankrupt and badly overdrawn in the Bank of

Heaven when suddenly we discovered Someone had put more grace in our account.

In a fallen world we should not be surprised that we fall flat on our faces from time to time. It's what you do after you fall that makes all the difference. Remember, with God's help you can get back up and start moving in the right direction again.

Lord Jesus, You are a wonderful Savior. May I never delay when You call me to take another step toward the light. Amen.

How would you chart your spiritual growth over the last five years? In what areas would you most like to grow in the next five years?

Name several ways in which you have experienced God's grace recently.

PROVIDENCE

❊

The Invisible Hand of God

The lot is cast into the lap, but its every decision is from the Lord.

Proverbs 16:33

Although the term *providence* is not found in most modern translations of the Bible, the concept is certainly biblical. It refers to "God's gracious oversight of the universe," which means that He upholds all things, governs all events, and directs everything to its appointed end, all the time and in every circumstance, always for His own glory.

The doctrine of God's providence teaches us several important truths. *First, God cares about the tiniest details of life.* He knows when a sparrow falls, and He numbers the hairs on your head. He keeps track of the stars in the skies and the rivers that flow to the oceans. He sets the day of your birth and the day of your death, and He ordains everything that comes to pass in between. *Second, He uses everything and wastes nothing.* There are no accidents with God, only incidents. This includes events that seem to us to be senseless tragedies. *Third, God's ultimate purpose is to shape His children into the image of Jesus [Christ]* (Romans 8:29). He often uses difficult moments and human tragedies to accomplish that purpose.

Many verses in the Bible teach these truths, including Acts 17:28 ("in him we live and move and have our being"); Colossians 1:17 ("in him all things hold together"); Hebrews 1:3 ("sustaining all things by his powerful word"); and especially Psalm 115:3, "Our God is in heaven; he does whatever pleases him."

When a cowboy applied for health insurance, the agent routinely asked if he had had any accidents during the previous year. The cowboy replied, "No. But I was bitten by a rattlesnake, and a horse kicked me in the ribs. That laid me up for a while." The agent said, "Weren't those accidents?" "No," replied the cowboy, "they did it on purpose." The cowboy realized that there are no such things as "accidents." How about you, Christian? Do you believe that some things catch God by surprise?

If we understand God's providence, it will set us free from bitterness. Like Joseph, we will be able to say, "You meant evil against me, but God meant it for good" (Genesis 50:20, NKJV). It will give us a new perspective on the tragedies of life. Not that we will always understand why bad things happen—often we won't. But providence teaches us that God is involved, for we know that "all things work together for good" for the children of God.

A friend came to my office recently with the sad news that his marriage was over. The details don't matter, but his reaction was worth noting. After wiping away the tears, he told me about a Christian song he had been listening to. He said it contained one statement that sustained him during the worst moments: "Life is hard but God is good."

In the end, we are all forced to make a choice. Either we believe that or we don't. We all know that life is hard. The doctrine of providence assures us that even in the worst moments of life God is good.

> *Give me, O Lord, a large supply of Your grace so that I may submit to You in every trial and trust You even when walking in the darkness. Amen.*

How do you reconcile the truth of God's providence with the truth of human responsibility for our own actions?

What does it mean to you to say that "God is good all the time"?

PRUDENCE

✦

Street Smarts

For giving prudence to the simple, knowledge and discretion to the young.

Proverbs 1:4

*P*rudence is a word that has almost fallen out of contemporary usage. Partly that is due to some unfortunate connections with concepts of cleverness and undue caution that have been associated with it. However, prudence was first on the list of the classic virtues, combining confidence, wisdom, enterprise, and ingenuity.

Essentially, prudence is the ability to make wise choices in the midst of your daily affairs. The word *prudent* means to be shrewd and clever in a positive sense. It means possessing street smarts. If you have a problem, you know how to get out of it. A person who has prudence is clever and shrewd in the ways of the world. He knows how to do things that need to be done. Solomon defines this in verse 3 as "doing what is right and just and fair." So it's not just how to do things, but how to do the right things in the right way.

Notice the two groups in verse 4. There are the simple and there are the young. Who are the simple? This term does not refer to IQ or overall mental ability. In the Bible, the word *simple* refers to people who are naive or gullible. Here's a short character profile of biblical simpletons. They are easily tricked because they lack discernment. They have "sucker" written all over their faces. And they make the same dumb mistakes over and over. They get into the same bad relationships over and over. They make the same bad investments over and over. They say the same foolish things over and over, they hurt their friends the same way, they make promises they break, they start out trying to do something but bite off more than they can chew and then have to back off. Maybe you know somebody like that, or maybe you are like that. If you gain prudence, you will learn how to break the cycle of making the same mistakes over and over.

If you follow the Lord from your youth, by the time you're old you'll be wise. You may start off foolish, simple, and gullible, but by the end you'll be prudent and disciplined and wise. By the time you're forty or fifty, you ought to have some street smarts. There is no excuse for being gullible when you're forty-five. It is not a matter of age, for I have known some seventy-five-year-olds who are really quite gullible. They are making the same mistakes they made when they were twenty-five. It's not strictly chronological, but the older you get, the wiser you ought to become. When you are young, you just don't know enough yet, you haven't lived enough, you haven't seen enough of life yet to be really experienced in street smarts.

No one becomes prudent overnight. But there is

hope for all of us, especially for the young. You may be a gullible fool, but you definitely don't have to stay that way.

Lord, help me to learn from my mistakes so that I won't have to make them all over again. Amen.

Name someone you know who makes the same mistakes over and over. What seems to be at the heart of the problem?

What mistakes are you continuing to make? What do you need to do about it?

PUNCTUALITY

❖

On Time Every Time

As vinegar to the teeth and smoke to the eyes, so is a sluggard to those who send him.

Proverbs 10:26

If you've ever sipped raw vinegar or stood downwind from a campfire, you know exactly what Solomon means. Raw vinegar is so sour it sets the teeth on edge. Hot smoke irritates the eyes. That's what a sluggard is like when you send him to do a job.

This poor fellow has several problems. He doesn't understand why you want *him* when you could have chosen old Joe at the next desk. He's not very interested in delivering the message because it doesn't seem important to him. He's not sure of the address, and besides that, it's nearly lunchtime, so he's bound to stop for an hour or so at the local hamburger joint. What should have been a short trip ends up taking the entire day. No wonder the boss gets ulcers just thinking about it.

What is the cure for such deliberate procrastination? To do your work as if God were watching—because He is. Colossians 3:23 reminds us that "whatever you do, work at it with all your heart, as working for the Lord, not for men." What does it mean—"working for the Lord"? It means understanding that every deed—whether small or large—is done for Him and in His name. His reputation is at stake when you show up at work fifteen minutes late or leave ten minutes early. People draw conclusions about the Lord Jesus from the way you do your work each day. If you do just enough to slide by but never enough to satisfy your employer, you are like raw vinegar to the teeth and hot smoke to the eyes—an irritation and not a blessing.

Sometimes we hear it said, "Don't sweat the small stuff." That's good advice if it simply means, "Focus on the things that really matter." But for the Christian on the job, there is no "small stuff." Details matter, deadlines count, promises must be kept, assignments must be completed, orders must be filled, records kept, and bills paid.

Punctuality is not the highest or most important issue in life. But it's not in the bottom ten, either. It matters more than we think. Some of us may have a lousy reputation simply because we don't do our jobs in a timely fashion.

Someone has pointed out that Jesus provides the perfect picture of a man who was never in haste, yet never missed an appointment. Because He was totally committed to doing His Father's will, He moved with purposeful dignity from one place to another.

Here is a good model for life. If you want to do the will of God on your job, a good place to begin is by showing up on time every time. Others will notice, our Lord will be honored, and you will find that punctuality brings its own reward.

Help me to be like Jesus, who was never in a hurry, never early, never late, but always on time. Amen.

Are you a punctual person? Can you be counted on to be on time every time? Why or why not? What excuses do you make for being late or missing an appointment?

Does your procrastination bother you? If so, what do you plan to do about it? If it doesn't bother you, please reread this section.

PURITY

✦

Staying Clean in a Dirty World

Say to wisdom, "You are my sister," and call understanding
your kinsman; they will keep you from the adulteress, from
the wayward wife with her seductive words.

Proverbs 7:4–5

Solomon felt so strongly about the dangers of sexual
temptation that he devoted three chapters of Proverbs
(5–7) to this subject. Three thousand years have passed
and his words still ring true. How can we stay pure in a
very dirty world? There are four decisions you must
make.

First, you must purposely avoid lust-producing situa-
tions. This is an extremely personal matter. Each one
must know his own limits. What produces lust in my life
may bore you. What makes you think impure thoughts
may put me to sleep. That's why it's hard to draw absolute
limits. But there is a line you must not cross. Make sure
you know where that line is for you—and then make sure
you don't cross it!

Second, you must purposely avoid provoking lust in oth-
er people. This is another very sensitive area. Sometimes
we Christians act as if freedom in Christ means we no
longer need to worry about how other people think or
feel. But that's not true. We have to be concerned about

the way we dress, but purity in this area also involves our language and our casual physical contact. It even includes our facial language—the smile, the glance, the wink, the knowing look. The rule is simple: Don't lead other people on! Don't be a tease! Don't be a flirt! Even if "nothing" happens, you have defrauded the other person.

Third, you must purposely choose purity. The decision to choose purity must be made in advance, based on a daily walk with God and grounded in a life of healthy activity.

So many people think Christianity is prudish. Far from it. *Christianity is not prudish, but it is modest and clean.* This week I ran across a striking sentence: "The way to clean out a stable is not with a shovel but with the Mississippi River." Nothing will clean out the corners of your life like a commitment to a life filled with wholesome activity. *When the "Dos" outweigh the "Don'ts," you will begin to experience the joy of purity and the thrill of victory.*

But you must make the choice! Not just once—but every single day—and often you must make the choice many times a day.

Fourth, you must be honest about your personal struggles. Lust is such a tricky matter that you will never win the victory on your own. Let me say that again: *You will never win the victory over lust simply by praying by yourself.* God never intended you to fight this battle alone.

Find a friend or a small group of friends and ask them to hold you accountable. Tell them you want them to ask you hard questions. Tell them not to let you off easily. Ask them to be tough enough so that you can't get by with sin.

The temptation to sexual impurity is very real. A man would be a fool to deny it. But you can stay clean—even in this dirty world—if you are willing to pay the price.

Heavenly Father, purify my heart, so that I will be clean from the inside out. Amen.

Which one of the four decisions do you most need to make right now? Who do you need to tell about the decision you are making?

What does it mean to you to purposely choose purity?

REBUKE

❖

Caring Enough to Tell the Truth

Better is open rebuke than hidden love. Wounds from a friend can be trusted, but an enemy multiplies kisses.

Proverbs 27:5–6

The King James Version says it elegantly: "Faithful are the wounds of a friend." Being a man or woman of integrity means that you don't walk away from a problem. It means that when you see a problem you hit it head-on, even though it would be easier and more convenient and pleasant just to walk away.

When someone asked General Norman Schwarzkopf the secret of his success, he replied very simply, "I never walk past a problem." Another friend put it this way: "Just remember, when it comes to solving problems, the first price you pay is always the cheapest." We ignore problems, hoping they will go away, but that rarely happens. And the price of solving them goes up, not down.

That last bit of advice came from a pastor who stayed in the same church over thirty years. He said, "I learned years ago when I was just starting out in the ministry that my tendency when I saw a problem was to just walk away. I discovered that I had to fight that tendency. I discovered through hard experience that the first price you pay is always the cheapest." The reason we don't want to get involved in solving problems we see around us is that we think if we just wait, the problems will solve themselves. That is rarely the case. Problems never get better when you ignore them. You may think you love someone too much to say anything. No, if you really loved them, you would speak the truth. You would speak it in love, but you will speak the truth he needs to hear. Integrity does not ignore the problems of life.

This truth has two sides. We are to love each other enough that we are willing for our brothers and sisters to hurt us if necessary. What does that mean? *It means that in the body of Christ we are to have some friends gathered around us who are close enough to hurt us from time to time.*

Does that sound like a shocking statement? It might seem that way. Nobody wants to be hurt by his friends. We all want to be surrounded by people who will make us feel better about ourselves. The very idea of having friends who will hurt us seems absurd. Friends don't hurt each other. Friends build each other up.

But that's not the whole story. If you want to live in a world where no one will ever hurt you, you picked the wrong planet on which to be born.

Spiritual growth becomes possible when you let other people get close enough to you to say the things to you that you need to hear—whether you want to hear them or not.

Lord Jesus, give me the courage I need to speak hard truth to my friends and the grace to receive it if they need to speak it to me. Amen.

Which is harder for you—to speak hard truth or to have someone speak it to you? Why?

What "hard truth" do you need to say that you have been putting off? What do you plan to do about it?

RESTLESSNESS

❖

Running Away from Your Problems

Like a bird that strays from its nest is a man who strays from his home.

Proverbs 27:8

This verse speaks to the desire we all feel from time to time to run away from our problems. The translators use various phrases to express this truth. The man in question "wanders far from home," he "strays from where he belongs," and he is "moved from his place."

The point of the comparison is not hard to find. All birds leave the nest eventually. But a bird that "strays" from the nest is abandoning its responsibilities and may end up never finding the way back home again. Even so, a man who "strays from where he belongs," especially from his home, loses touch with the most important realities of life. God gave us families so that we would have roots. In the words of Robert Frost, "Home is where, when you go there, they have to take you in." But where will a man go if he strays from the "nest" God has given him?

This certainly applies to men and woman who leave their mates and children in search of happiness. But it also applies to the general temptation to believe that the grass is always greener on the other side of the fence.

Thus we hop from job to job, looking for the one place where we (and our careers) will blossom. We migrate from church to church, stopping only long enough to see the blemishes in each congregation but not long enough to make lasting friendships. In the same vein, we move from house to house and town to town, flying like a stray bird farther and farther from our roots. Sometimes we ditch our lifetime friends in favor of new ones.

One important point must be emphasized. Leaving is not wrong, nor is changing jobs, starting over, moving to a new community, or finding a new church. Sometimes we must break a friendship for our own spiritual well-being. But motive is all important. Leaving and changing and making a new start can sometimes be nothing more than a convenient excuse for running from our problems.

Often we stray because we expected to be happy, and when we aren't, we pack up and leave. But marriage is tough at times, even the best friends get on your nerves, no job is perfect, no church is always harmonious, and life in general can be boring and unpredictable.

So what? If you cop out and drop out, do you really think things will get better? If you are running from your problems, running away won't make things better. One mark of maturity is that you can face your problems head-on, without flinching, without making excuses, without complaining, and without running away.

God has a purpose in allowing us to struggle with the temptation to run away. *He is developing character in us, and to do that, adversity is essential.* That's why life isn't easy, why nothing works the way it's supposed to, why we struggle so hard to get ahead. God's agenda and His timetable are often quite different from ours.

Do not despair. The road is hard and the journey long because God made it that way. But there's a crown and a throne at the end for those who persevere.

Lord, help me to stay in my nest until You tell me it's time to leave. Amen.

When are you most tempted to run away from your problems? From your perspective, what is the difference between responsible leaving and running away?

What situation, person, or problem are you most tempted to run away from right now?

REVENGE

✳

Let God Get Even

Do not say, "I'll do to him as he has done to me; I'll pay that man back for what he did."

Proverbs 24:29

There is a man in the Bible who had every right to be angry at the way he was treated. *He was a good man, a teacher of God's law, a man who helped those in need and got angry only when he saw injustice in the world.* When he started his ministry, the powers that be at first found him a nuisance and later a threat. Eventually, they decided that he must be killed. But because he was popular with the common people, they couldn't arrest him haphazardly. They had to find a plausible excuse that would give them a cover for their dirty deeds.

The day came when he traveled to the capital city for a public celebration. That's when the leaders made their move. They had found a man among his followers—his treasurer, no less—who was willing to sell him out in exchange for a handful of money. The deal was struck, the time set, the plan made. It all went like clockwork, and the good man was arrested.

Outside the city walls, near a limestone quarry with the strange face of a skull outlined on the side of a cliff, *the good man was put to death.* He didn't say much that day, only about seven or eight sentences. But, oh, what words they were. What power! What truth he spoke!

Do you remember the first words he said from the cross? How could you ever forget them? He looked down, his chest heaving, the sun beating down on his fevered, bleeding brow, his face a mass of blood and tears, his hands and feet dripping blood from the nail holes. He saw the laughter, heard the jeers, and knew that they were laughing at him.

He had done nothing wrong. Nothing to deserve this.

He closed his eyes, as if in prayer. Then he looked again at the howling, wild mob. *"Father, forgive them, for they do not know what they are doing"* (Luke 23:34).

Forgive them? But they were guilty of the greatest crime in all history.

Forgive them? But he was innocent—and they knew it.

Forgive them! But they had twisted the truth, made up lies, slandered his name, bribed his treasurer, rigged the trial, and guaranteed his death. It was murder, pure and simple. They meant to kill him—and they did.

Forgive them? How could it be?

But that's what he said. *"Father, forgive them."* He was a good man, the best man the world has ever seen. He came to show us how to live, and he came to show us how to die. He came to save us while we were yet sinners. *He even came to save those who put him to death.*

"Father, forgive them." I'm so glad Jesus said that, because it shows us that forgiveness is always possible. If He could forgive, then anything is possible. If the Son of God could rise above revenge, if He could find a way to forgive His enemies, then so can we.

> *Lord Jesus, thank You for showing us how to forgive the unforgivable. Now please help me to do it. Amen.*

Name three people you'd like to get even with right now. Can you think of anyone who would like to get even with you?

What would need to change in your heart before you could truly and sincerely forgive your enemies? Are you willing for God to make that change?

RIGHTEOUSNESS

❋

If You Want It, You Can Have It

He who pursues righteousness and love finds life, prosperity and honor.

Proverbs 21:21

Whatever you seek in life, you tend to find. It may be sexual pleasure or financial gain or personal happiness. Or it may be something higher and better. In this case Solomon tells us that if we want life, prosperity, and honor (and who doesn't?), we can have it. But you don't receive those things by seeking after them. Seek *righteousness!* And everything else you desire will be added to you. If that reminds you of Matthew 6:33, it should. This is the Old Testament version of that famous verse.

The tragedy of our time is that so many people are wasting their lives chasing after three things that can never satisfy—money, sex, and power. We want money, so we sacrifice *our families* to get it. We want sex, so we sacrifice *our morals* to get it. We want power, so we sacrifice *our friends* to get it.

If you want righteousness, you can have it. Let me go out on a limb and make a bold statement. *Whatever you want in the spiritual realm, you can have if you want it badly enough.*

- If you want it, you can have a close walk with God.
- If you want it, you can have a better marriage.
- If you want to, you can do God's will.
- If you want to, you can grow spiritually.
- If you want to, you can become a man of God or a woman of God.
- If you want to, you can change deeply ingrained habits.
- If you want to, you can break destructive patterns of behavior.

There is a "God-shaped vacuum" inside every human heart. Since nature abhors a vacuum, if we don't fill it with God, we will fill it with something else. So many of us have filled our hearts with the junk food of the world. No wonder we are so unhappy. No wonder we jump from one job to another and from one relationship to another.

We're like little children who won't let go of the marble in order to receive a diamond. "No, I won't give up my weekend affair for eternal joy." "Trade a broken marriage and a failed career for peace and forgiveness? Forget it!" "Give up my drug addiction and be forgiven for all my sins? No way, man." "You say I can replace my anger and bitterness with peace and contentment? I can't take the chance. Sorry."

No wonder we stay the way we are. We're trapped in the pit of a thousand excuses. We'd rather have misery and pain than risk it all on Jesus.

Sixteen hundred years ago Saint Augustine explained both the problem and the solution: "O God, you have made us for yourself, and our hearts are restless until they find rest in you." *You will never be happy until you put God first in your life.* And you can never do that until you surrender your life to Jesus Christ once and for all.

In the kingdom of God everything begins with a seeking heart!

> *O God, I hunger and thirst to know You better. May I be less pleased with what I am that I may become all You want me to be. Amen.*

Are you pursuing righteousness with all your heart? If the answer is no, what are you pursuing instead of righteousness?

Are you ready to risk it all on Jesus?

SATISFACTION

---❖---

Living Above Your Circumstances

The fear of the Lord leads to life: Then one rests content, untouched by trouble.

Proverbs 19:23

To fear the Lord means living in the light of His presence. Those who truly fear God respect Him and live by His principles. They never forget that He is watching everything they do and weighing all their words and deeds. While that might seem oppressive to some, Solomon tells us that this is the only way to real life. When you respect the Lord, you are content no matter what happens to you. Though circumstances may overwhelm you, the center of life is "untouched by trouble."

Not long ago I received a letter from a friend in Florida who wrote to tell me about an unexpected change of plans in his life. Suddenly his future was not as certain as he thought it was. To make things worse, the change of plans was not definite. Things might change or they might not. But he wouldn't know for a few months, so he couldn't do anything other than wait. That's a frustrating position to be in.

I found his response invigorating. His letter described his dilemma and then included this sentence: "I guess I'll have to be happy no matter what happens, so I will."

It's that last phrase that grips the mind: "So I will." When I read those words, I stopped and said to myself, *What a great way of looking at life.* So many of us get grumpy when our plans are waylaid by unexpected circumstances. I know people who lose their religion if they hit a traffic jam or don't have enough change to buy a newspaper. How easy for all of us to let circumstances dictate our moods. When things are going great, we feel great. When life is tough, we're grouchy and mean-spirited.

I think it was Abraham Lincoln who said, "Most people are as happy as they want to be." Happiness is a choice. Each day when we roll out of bed we're faced with a profound choice: Will we face this day with optimism, courage, and a positive spirit, or will we give up and start complaining because someone forgot to put the cap on the toothpaste? Think about it. How many days are ruined before they begin because we have chosen (yes, chosen) to focus on the irritations of life?

In using such trivial events I don't mean to downplay the truly great problems of life—sickness, the loss of a job, a wrecked car, an angry boss, impending surgery, and so on. But most of us face those things infrequently. Traffic jams are a daily reality for most of us. The same with mislaid scissors, handprints on the wall, overdue bills, and discovering at 6 A.M. that you've run out of milk and Peanut Butter Cap'n Crunch. These are the true tests of character.

I think my friend is on to something. "I guess I'll have to be happy no matter what happens, so I will." This is a step beyond *que sera, sera,* because the secret of happiness is not simply accepting what happens, but choosing to be happy in the midst of the unplanned surprises of life.

You have a choice to make. If you fear the Lord, you can be content no matter what happens.

Ruler of my life, help me to choose happiness today. Amen.

How can one be "untouched" by trouble even in the midst of overwhelming difficulty?

Did you "choose happiness" today? If so, how has the day gone? If not, what does that say about your relationship with God?

Do you fear God enough to be happy?

SECURITY

✦

Hope Beyond the Grave

When calamity comes, the wicked are brought down, but even in death the righteous have a refuge.

Proverbs 14:32

Sometimes it is amazing how much you can learn from your children. Many years ago, when our oldest son was not quite four years old, my wife asked him how people get to heaven when they die. She thought he would say, "Jesus takes us there," or some reasonable facsimile.

Joshua, however, had other ideas. He said, "When we die, there's a ladder and we climb on it up to heaven." A few days later, Marlene asked again, "Joshua, how do people get to heaven when they die?" He stopped to think about it for a while. Then he smiled real big, the way you do when you know you've figured out the answer to a tough question. "I know. When we die, God lets down a vacuum and sucks us up to heaven." This answer sounded a little closer to the truth.

Several more days passed. We visited a shopping mall and Marlene asked once again, "Joshua, how do people get to heaven when they die?" This one is easy. "They ride up on an escalator." End of quiz.

Actually, there's something to be said for each answer. After all, the Bible speaks of Jacob's ladder, and a vacuum does sound something like the rapture. But an escalator? Maybe he had been watching one of those commercials where the two angels escort a man up to the clouds and on to heaven.

Later, I asked Joshua again. This time he said, "I don't know." Then he gave the best answer of all, "Let me ask Mom." So he did, and she just smiled at him.

There are many mysteries to the Christian faith, and one of them is how we get to heaven when we die. It's just as well that we don't know the answer. We probably couldn't understand it anyway.

I tried one last question. "Joshua, who do you have to believe in to go to heaven?" That one was easy. "Jesus!"

In the end, it will not be what we know but who we know that makes the difference. If we know Jesus, we shall go to heaven. If we do not know Him, how we get there will make no difference because we won't be making the trip

John Wesley, the father of Methodism, was fond of saying, "Our people die well." He meant that Christians face death with a confidence the world cannot understand. Put simply, we aren't afraid to die. While we may fear the circumstances of our death, we aren't worried about what happens afterward. We know that to be absent from the body is to be present with the Lord.

What does it all mean? The Bible says that we Christians sorrow, but not as those "who have no hope" (1 Thessalonians 4:13). Death will never be easy, but for those who believe in Jesus it is nothing to be feared. If Jesus has taken us this far, He will not abandon us when we need Him most.

Lord Jesus, thank You for taking the sting out of death and setting us free to live without fear. Amen.

How much longer do you expect to live?

Are you afraid to die? Are you ready to die? If you're not ready to die, what do you need to do to be prepared when the moment comes?

SELF-CONTROL

❖

Learn This or Else!

A quick-tempered man does foolish things, and a crafty man is hated.

Proverbs 14:17

The Bible offers many examples of men who failed because they lacked this essential element of self-control. But no one sticks in my mind like Samson, the undisputed heavyweight champion of ancient Israel. His story is found in Judges 13–16 (that's in the "White Pages" section of your Bible, the part you don't read very often). But we ought to read about Samson more often than we do, for his life is filled with lessons, examples, and applications.

In one sense, Samson is one of the best-known heroes in all the Bible. Generations of children have marveled at the story of Samson defeating the Philistines with the jawbone of an ass. Many teenagers know about Samson's long hair and how Delilah tricked the secret of his strength from him. Most of us know that he had his eyes poked out, and that he died pushing the pillars of the Philistine temple apart, collapsing the building, taking with him to their death thousands of Philistines. If you go to church at all, you know Samson. His is a story both heroic and tragic.

When we read Samson's story, we tend to think that his problems were all in the sexual area. But that ignores the deeper reality that time and again Samson made foolish decisions because his emotions got the best of him. Sometimes he lost his temper; other times he took unreasonable chances in order to get even; often he seemed irresistibly attracted to Philistine women.

First he is filled with lust and then he is filled with anger. Then he's full of lust again, then anger again, and then lust and anger again. He's riding an emotional roller coaster, from the peak to the valley and around a sharp corner, and then he does it all over again. One moment he's worshiping God; the next, he's flirting with the Philistine women. On one occasion he leads the army of Israel to a stunning military victory by the power of the Holy Spirit. Later he sleeps with a Philistine prostitute. Not long after that he meets Delilah, who tricks him into revealing the secret of his power, which leads to his imprisonment and death.

Samson never learned to control his emotions, and so they controlled him completely. Proverbs 16:32 could have been written about Samson: "Better a patient man than a warrior, a man who controls his temper than one who takes a city." In his day, Samson had taken more than one city. But he never learned to control his temper. He never learned how to rule his spirit. He never knew the first thing about self-control. In the end, his runaway emotions ran away with him.

The same thing can happen to any of us. Self-control

is impossible without the Holy Spirit. You can have the Holy Spirit in control, or your emotions can take control. There is no third option and no middle ground.

There's a little Samson in all of us. Learn this lesson well. Without the help of the Holy Spirit, we're all doomed to follow in the same path of self-destruction.

Holy Spirit, I'm ready for You to take control of my life. Please fill me with Your power so that I might become a truly different person. Amen.

Why is self-control such a valuable character trait? What are the marks of a person without self-control?

In what areas of your life do you most need to develop this character quality?

SILENCE

❖

A Fool's Best Friend

Even a fool is thought wise if he keeps silent, and discerning if he holds his tongue.

Proverbs 17:28

This certainly is one of the most encouraging proverbs. It offers hope for all of us who basically make our living with words. Here are a few other verses on this same subject: "When words are many, sin is not absent, but he who holds his tongue is wise" (10:19). "A man of understanding holds his tongue" (11:12b). "He who guards his lips guards his life, but he who speaks rashly will come to ruin" (13:3). "He who guards his mouth and his tongue keeps himself from calamity" (21:23).

Truth-telling begins with silence. Speak less and you will speak more truthfully. The more you say, the more likely you are to exaggerate, slander, mislead, and stretch the truth.

A few years ago I heard a man say, "Feel free to have no opinion on that." What a novel thought—"Feel free to have no opinion." I think that struck me because in my younger, brasher days I felt like I should be ready to discourse intelligently on any subject. Ask a question and I was ready with an answer, an opinion, or an argument. With the passing of a few years and my entrance into mid-life, I now understand that there are many areas about which I know nothing. For instance, if you ask a question about the history of China, I don't know enough to make a useful contribution. Maybe someday I'll know more about China than I do right now, but for the moment, I'm better off not opening my mouth.

Here's a liberating thought. It's OK not to know all the answers. It's also OK not to offer an opinion on every passing fad. You don't have to dominate every conversation or try to be an expert on everything. You can't, you aren't, and everyone knows it; and if you try to fake it, eventually you'll be caught up short by someone who really does know what they're talking about.

I think it was Calvin Coolidge who declared that he never got into trouble for something he didn't say. While I wouldn't care to press that to the extreme (after all, there are times when silence is wrong), his point is still well taken. Say less, but make your words count.

For those who talk for a living (and for the rest of us as well), why not try "creative listening"? *It means praying while you are listening.* Most of us don't listen very well anyway. When someone else is talking, we're busy trying to figure out what we're going to say next. No wonder we don't communicate!

Creative silence means listening more, saying less, and praying instead of interrupting.

Pray for wisdom!

Pray for God's guidance!

Pray for understanding!

Pray for God's love to be manifested in your speech!

The Bible is clear on this point. The more we speak, the less truth we tell. If we want to become more truthful, the first step is to speak less.

Father, make me like Jesus, who spoke for the ages and never wasted a word. Amen.

Do you talk too much? How would your friends answer that question?

Name three things in life you've decided to have no opinion about. Why is this important?

Can you think of a situation recently where you would have been better off if you had talked less?

SIMPLICITY

❖

Learning to Live with Less

Better a little with righteousness than much gain with injustice.

Proverbs 16:8

Most of us live on the opposite principle. We figure our contentment on the basis of how many of our needs are met. Unfortunately, it's hard to reach a place where all our needs are constantly met. By that standard, it's hard to ever really be content. If contentment is measured by how much of the world's goods you possess, who can ever say, "I have enough"? Someone asked a multimillionaire when he was going to stop working. "When I make enough money," he replied. "How much money is enough?" "Just one more dollar."

That's the way most of us figure contentment. In our hearts we think, *I would be happy if only I had a new car or a new job or a new dress or a new husband or a new wife.* Since life is hardly ever that simple, we stay frustrated when we ought to be happy.

No wonder we are never satisfied. Instead of being weaned from the world, we are wedded to it. Or maybe I should say, *welded* to it. In any case, our soul is anything but quiet; our countenance, anything but peaceful.

How does God go about weaning us from our dependence on the things of the world? I ran across a three-part answer from a Bible commentator writing over a century ago. *First*, God makes the things of the world bitter to us. *Second*, He removes one by one the things on which we depend. *Third*, He gives us something better. *In the end, we find that we no longer need the things we used to think we couldn't do without.* And our walk with God is stronger than ever before.

Most of us have made a list of our blessings—especially at Thanksgiving. When we make that list, we normally emphasize our material blessings. That's good and proper but it doesn't exhaust the subject.

Here's a simple suggestion. Make a list of the things which, through suffering and hardship, God has taken away from you in the last twelve months. And now your faith is stronger and deeper. And now your walk with God means more than it ever did before.

I want you to list those things you used to think you couldn't live without but now you know you can. It could be a dream you had for your life that consumed all your energy, but God has taken it from you and you have found, "Yes, I can live without that." It might be a relationship or a job or a prized possession. What have you learned that you can do without and still be happy?

As the song says, "Count your many blessings—name them one by one, and it will surprise you what the Lord hath done." The surprise is not just in the outward material blessings of the last year. It is also in the times of pain and suffering that seemed to be for no good purpose but turned out to be blessings in disguise. That, too, is the goodness and grace of God.

Lord, I thank You for the things I no longer have to have in order to be happy. Amen.

Make a list of things you have discovered you can now live without. What does that list teach you about the Lord? Yourself?

What things/relationships do you still think you must have in order to be happy?

SLOTH

---
*

An Underestimated Sin

The sluggard buries his hand in the dish; he will not even bring it back to his mouth!

Proverbs 19:24

Here is a picture both sad and silly: A grown man so lazy he won't even lift his food to his mouth. He just bends over and buries his face in the mashed potatoes. With the means of nourishment right in front of him, the sluggard is too sleepy to eat.

Solomon offers many other warnings in Proverbs about the sluggard. He won't take advantage of his opportunities: "A sluggard does not plow in season; so at harvest time he looks but finds nothing" (20:4). He loves his bed: "Do not love sleep or you will grow poor; stay awake and you will have food to spare" (20:13). He refuses to work even though he is filled with unsatisfied desire: "The sluggard's craving will be the death of him, because his hands refuse to work. All day long he craves for more, but the righteous give without sparing" (21:25–26). He makes silly excuses: "The sluggard says, 'There is a lion outside!' or 'I will be murdered in the streets!'" (22:13). He can't finish a job: "The lazy man does not roast his game, but the diligent man prizes his possessions" (12:27). In his conceit he believes he is wiser than those fellows who work hard: "The sluggard is wiser in his own eyes than seven men who answer discreetly" (26:16). As a consequence, he never accomplishes anything: "The way of the sluggard is blocked with thorns, but the path of the upright is a highway" (15:19). And he is an enormous annoyance to anyone who hires him: "As vinegar to the teeth and smoke to the eyes, so is a sluggard to those who send him" (10:26). The poorhouse is his final destination: "A little sleep, a little slumber, a little folding of the hands to rest—and poverty will come on you like a bandit and scarcity like an armed man" (24:33–34).

Sloth comes in many forms, but perhaps most commonly in the unfinished projects of life. We get a job and can't keep it. We start a book and don't finish it. We begin a job around the house but don't complete it. We start a list but don't finish it. We switch from this to that. We play here awhile, there awhile, and then somewhere else awhile. Always changing, always restless, never able to see anything through to the end. We do the minimum required and barely slide by.

Here is the application. What do you need to do this week that is undone in your life? It will take you less than three seconds to answer that question. Now that you know what it is, name it. Plan it. Schedule it. Do it. *This week.* Don't put it off. Stop making excuses.

It is not for nothing that sloth was counted as one of the seven deadly sins. You want to rest? You will have time later. Go out to the cemetery. There is not much work out there. Until then, get busy doing what needs to be done.

Lord Jesus, help me to do what needs to be done today and to do it with gusto. Amen.

What do you need to do this week that is undone in your life? What do you plan to do about it?

How many unfinished things are there in your life right now?

SOBRIETY

---❖---

Knowing When to Say No

Wine is a mocker and beer a brawler; whoever is led astray by them is not wise.

Proverbs 20:1

There are a great many references to wine, strong drink, and drunkenness scattered throughout the Bible. The earliest reference is in Genesis; the last, in Revelation. The total number of verses would run up into the hundreds. However, there is not a binding rule, i.e., "Thou shalt not drink." In one place, the Bible says, "Do not get drunk on wine" (Ephesians 5:18). In another place, the Bible speaks of "wine that gladdens the heart of man" (Psalm 104:15). In one place, Paul says that no drunkard shall inherit the kingdom of God (1 Corinthians 6:10). In another place, he advises Timothy to "use a little wine because of your stomach" (1 Timothy 5:23).

Because there is no universal rule, each believer must make his own decision guided by the larger teachings of Scripture, his own situation, the counsel of others, and common sense.

However, to put the matter that way does not exactly settle the issue, does it? A quick check of the concordance under the word *wine* shows that many of the references warn the reader of the negative effects of alcohol. Consider the following examples:

Proverbs 20:1: "Wine is a mocker and beer a brawler."

Isaiah 24:9: "The beer is bitter to its drinkers."

First Corinthians 6:10: "[No] drunkards . . . will inherit the kingdom of God."

Ephesians 5:18: "Do not get drunk on wine."

Galatians 5:19–21: "The acts of the sinful nature are obvious: . . . drunkenness."

First Peter 4:3: "For you have spent enough time in the past doing what pagans choose to do—living in debauchery, lust, drunkenness, orgies, carousing and detestable idolatry."

The Bible warns us repeatedly of the dangers of alcohol. Let's look at one other passage: Proverbs 23:29–35.

Who has woe? Who has sorrow? Who has strife? Who has complaints? Who has needless bruises? Who has bloodshot eyes? Those who linger over wine, who go to sample bowls of mixed wine. Do not gaze at wine when it is red, when it sparkles in the cup, when it goes down smoothly! In the end it bites like a snake and poisons like a viper. Your eyes will see strange sights and your mind imagine confusing things. You will be like one sleeping on the high seas, lying on top of the rigging. "They hit me," you will say, "but I'm not hurt! They beat me, but I don't feel it. When will I wake up so I can find another drink?"

What is the Bible telling us? That we cannot drink? No. That it's a sin to take a drink? No, not necessarily. It's telling us there's danger ahead. Think twice before you take the first drink.

Suppose you are traveling through the mountains and come to a fork in the road. One fork says "Safe for all travelers." The other is labeled "Dangerous road." Watch out for falling rocks. Soft shoulders. Landslides possible. Sharp curves, no guard rails. Travel at your own risk." Both roads are open, both offer scenic views, and you see cars going both ways. Which way are you going to go? *I suppose it depends on how ready you are to risk your own life.* Either way, you've got a choice to make.

> *Lord, give me wisdom in my personal decisions, knowing that others are influenced by the choices I make. Amen.*

What is your own personal practice regarding the use of alcohol? Are you comfortable with the decisions you have made?

Is there any history of alcohol abuse in your family or among your close friends? How does that impact your own decisions regarding alcohol?

SOVEREIGNTY

❖

God Has the Last Word

To man belong the plans of the heart, but from the Lord comes the reply of the tongue.

Proverbs 16:1

We might paraphrase this verse as follows: "A man can have his own ideas, but the Lord inspires the words he utters." This is a powerful reminder that God is in control. In the words of the Westminster Confession of Faith, "He ordains whatsoever comes to pass."

Romans 8:28 tells us that "in all things God works for the good of those who love him, who have been called according to his purpose." What does Romans 8:28 mean by "all things"? How inclusive is it? It is utterly inclusive. It includes all that can happen in the life of a child of God. It includes the good and the bad, health and sickness, wealth and poverty, the sunlight and the shadow, high noon and midnight, life and death. That means that Romans 8:28 is just as true in the hospital as it is in the sanctuary. It means that when you are in the waiting room and that clock will not move and you know your loved one is in the hands of a surgeon, that no matter the outcome, whether life or death, cancer or no cancer, whether you see her again or not, you know that moment is in God's hands. It is part of the "all things" that work together for good. There is nothing that can happen to the child of God that is outside of the "all things" of Romans 8:28.

Do we really believe that? There is no greater question facing men and women who believe in God. For every person who doubts the deity of Christ there are a hundred who secretly wonder about the goodness of God.

Skeptics put the matter this way. If God were all-powerful, He would stop the suffering in the world. If God were good, He would not permit such things to happen. Whichever path you choose, God ends up either too weak to stop evil or too callous to care.

The Bible presents God Himself as the great Sufferer who fully met the problem of evil in the gift of His own Son. I am reminded of the distraught father who cried out, "Where was God when my son died?" The answer came back, "The same place He was when His Son died."

How shall we deal with the unexplainable mysteries of life? When you look at a piece of fabric through a magnifying glass the edges are blurred while the middle is clear. Life is like a piece of fabric. Many times the edges are blurred; there are many circumstances we do not understand. But the center of life is clear, and in the center we find the Cross of Jesus Christ.

Most of the time we will never know the answer to the question "Why?" God never asks us to understand, but only to trust Him in spite of our doubts. Peace comes when we finally realize we don't have to have all the answers.

The edges of life will often be blurry, but the center is clear and it points to the Cross.

Father, if You gave Your Son for me, how can I ever doubt Your love for me? I can't, and I won't. Amen.

What does it mean to you to say that God is sovereign? List some of the positive and negative events that have "worked together" for good in your own life.

If you could ask God just one question about something that has happened in your life, what would it be?

SUBMISSION

❈

How God Works Through Others

The wise in heart accept commands, but a chattering fool comes to ruin.

Proverbs 10:8

Submission is one of the more difficult lessons to learn, especially when we have more wisdom than the person to whom we must submit. It's not that difficult to obey a person we admire greatly. Most of us will even obey people we don't like if they seem to know what they are talking about. But what do you do when you don't like the person, don't respect him, and truly believe he doesn't have a clue?

The temptation at that point is to become a "chattering fool." We talk back, we argue incessantly, we filibuster, we stonewall, we make excuses for not obeying, we stage a work slowdown, we gossip, we complain—we do everything but accept the commands of those in authority over us.

"But a chattering fool comes to ruin." Talking too much eventually gets us into trouble. We may end up losing our job or that promotion we coveted. It might mean that we irritate our superiors to the point that they take action against us.

Shouldn't we speak out when we have valid concerns?

Yes, of course. But there is a fundamental difference between expressing a concern and refusing to accept direction from others.

Behind the principle of submission stands the truth of God's providence. If you believe that God works through the details of life, then you must also believe that He has placed you exactly where you are right now for a particular purpose. Consider Joseph. First he was Jacob's favored son; then he found himself in a pit; then in Potiphar's house; then in prison. Finally he became prime minister of Egypt and, as a result, was reunited with the brothers who sold him into slavery. In the end he could confidently proclaim, "You meant evil against me, but God meant it for good" (Genesis 50:20, NKJV).

When everything else is stripped away, we are to accept commands from others because we believe in God, not because we believe in the person giving commands. He (or she) may or may not be a worthy person. We may in fact be more qualified. But that has nothing to do with how we respond. If we believe that God is in charge of where we are right now, we can obey with joy (if not with happiness), because we know with certainly that by receiving commands from others, we are ultimately obeying God—who definitely has more wisdom than we do.

This has very practical ramifications for Christian wives who struggle with the issue of submission to their husbands. In the light of God's providence, submission means believing that God is able to work through your husband to accomplish His will in your life, to protect your interests, and to meet your deepest needs. To state the matter this way does not answer every question, nor does it make submission easy, but at least it puts the matter in the proper context—not between a wife and her husband but ultimately between a woman and her God.

Submission to any human authority doesn't come naturally to any of us. But if we believe in God and His involvement in our lives, we can find the strength to submit when we're tempted to become chattering fools.

> *Lord, give me eyes to see Your invisible hand at work through those in authority over me. Amen.*

At what points in your life are you most tempted to talk back instead of obey?

How do you personally define the difference between expressing valid concerns and refusing to accept direction from others?

SUCCESS

✦

It All Begins with God

Commit to the Lord whatever you do, and your plans will succeed.

Proverbs 16:3

The word *commit* basically means "to roll." It was used of rolling large rocks over the mouth of a cave (Joshua 10:18), of garments rolled in blood (Isaiah 9:5), of the sky rolled up as a scroll (Isaiah 34:4), and of an army marching through a breach in the city wall (Job 30:14). To commit in this context means to proactively roll all our plans, our dreams, and our hopes over to the Lord. When you commit something to the Lord you are saying, "Lord, either I can take care of this or You can, and You're much better qualified to handle it, so I'm turning the whole thing over to You."

To put the matter that way brings us face-to-face with the third petition of the Lord's Prayer: "Your will be done on earth as it is in heaven" (Matthew 6:10). C. S. Lewis said that there are two kinds of people in the world, and only two kinds: those who say to God, "Thy will be done," and those to whom God says in the end, "Thy will be done." God has a will, and you have a will. To pray "Your will be done" is actually to pray "Lord, let my own will not be done if it in any way conflicts with

Your will." Those are easy words to say in theory, but difficult to apply to your cherished dreams and well-laid plans.

A friend of mine once came to me with a sobering message: "Ray, you're holding on too tightly. You've got to let go." When she said it, I mumbled something spiritual but I didn't believe her. It took me a year or more to see the truth.

My friend was right. I didn't want to let go. The thing I was holding on to meant everything to me. It was my baby, my dream, my future. I held on to it because I was deathly afraid to let go.

God eventually had to take it away from me. But, oh, it was painful. I fought and argued and wept. God paid no attention to my anger. He slowly and carefully pried my fingers away one by one. When He got down to the thumb, I fought Him with all my strength but to no avail. In the end He took back that which had always belonged to Him.

Does God have the right to be God in your life? You say, "Of course He does." Yes, but have you told Him so? Or do you feel the need to fight with God about His plans for you? Former Senate Chaplain Richard Halverson recounts a prayer he often heard Bob Pierce, founder of World Vision, pray: "Lord, I give you license to interfere in my life and plans at any time, in any way, at any cost." What a great way to approach life. "Lord, You're in charge. I've got my plans, my dreams, my personal agenda, but if You want to change things, go right ahead—and You don't have to tell me in advance."

That's precisely what it means to "commit" your way to the Lord. When you give God the right to be God in your life, you will experience true success, the kind that only He can give.

Father, I give You the right to interfere with my own plans if that is necessary so that Your will might be done in my life. Amen.

What are your dreams, hopes, and plans for the future? Have you ever rolled them over onto the Lord?

Are you holding on to anything too tightly right now?

TACT

✦

Making a Point
Without Making an Enemy

*Through patience a ruler can be persuaded, and a gentle
tongue can break a bone.*

Proverbs 25:15

Someone noted that tact is like a girdle. It enables you
to organize the awkward truth more attractively. A
Chinese proverb says it this way: Do not use a hatchet to
remove a fly from a friend's forehead.

Both those statements remind us that often we are
called up to say "hard truth" to others. Sometimes that
means risking the love of those we hold most dear. We
must tell them the truth or they will not get better. Perhaps they simply don't see it, or don't want to see it. They
may have a bad habit that is holding them back, or they
may have an unseen character flaw that causes them to
lose the respect of others. You know it, you see it, and you
care about them. Do you care enough to tell the truth?
Do you also care enough to speak with tact?

Proverbs 25:15 spells out two strategies you can use.
The first is patience. That means waiting till the right
moment to speak your mind. Timing is everything. If
you embarrass someone publicly, he isn't likely to respond

favorably. Likewise, if you ambush someone the moment he walks through the door, he will regard your words as a personal attack. So before you speak, take your time. Think. Pray. Ask God to give you an open door. When it comes, then you are ready for the second strategy.

Second, use a gentle tongue. Just as a "gentle answer turns away wrath" (15:1), even so a gentle tongue can break a bone. Here is the picture of a hardened bone being softened bit by bit by the touch of a gentle tongue. It won't happen quickly, but in most cases gentleness accomplishes far more than threats or intimidation.

In making a plea for tact, I am asking for nothing more than that we "[speak] the truth in love" (Ephesians 4:15). Jesus did it, and is remembered today as the supreme embodiment of love. Yet no one ever spoke the truth like He did. He wasn't afraid to speak truth to power, to challenge the rulers of His day. And when necessary He didn't hesitate to take a whip and clean out the temple—which doesn't sound like a very tactful thing to do. But He did it, and since He was the Son of God it must have been the right thing to do.

So what exactly is this gentle tongue that can break a bone? It is the ability to say the right thing at the right time in the right way without saying anything you didn't want to say and that didn't need to be said. A tactful person seeks to find a private place and a fitting moment. It means you refuse to dump all your frustrations on another person. You say what needs to be said in the quickest, kindest, most direct way possible. Then you move on.

Tact is really nothing more than wisdom applied to the "girdle moments" of life. Remember, when you have to speak the awkward truth, don't use a hatchet to get rid of a fly.

Lord Jesus, I pray for Your Spirit to fill my lips so that I might speak as You did. Amen.

Do you have trouble with tact? If in doubt, ask a friend and you'll get a quick answer.

What is the difference between tact and flattery? Between boldness and brusqueness? Why do we so often confuse them?

Give an example showing how tact helped you deal with a difficult situation. Or, looking back, you wish you had shown more tact than you did.

TEMPTATION

❋

Just Say No

My son, if sinners entice you, do not give in to them.

Proverbs 1:10

Playwright Oscar Wilde once jokingly remarked, "I can resist everything except temptation." We smile when we read those words because they speak an important truth about the human condition. Temptation pays a visit to each of us every day, and most of us struggle to say no.

Temptation is not new in any sense. Temptation is the same for us as it was for Adam and Eve in the Garden of Eden. Satan tempts us today in the same way he tempted Jesus in the wilderness. From the very beginning, a battle has raged for the souls of men and women, a battle that touches all of us sooner or later.

Think how many temptations you and I face in an ordinary day. Staying in bed late—the temptation to laziness. Dressing carelessly—the temptation to sloppiness. Growling at the breakfast table—the temptation to unkindness. Arguing over who should change the baby this time—the temptation to selfishness. Starting work ten minutes late—the temptation to slothfulness. Losing your temper when a co-worker crashes your computer—the temptation to impatience. Flirting with that good-looking woman, taking a second look at that good-looking man—the temptation to lust. Refusing to speak to a person who has hurt you—the temptation to malice. Repeating a juicy story of your neighbor's misfortune—the temptation to gossip. Taking a secret drink at a party—the temptation to drunkenness. Lying awake at night thinking sensual thoughts—the temptation to impurity. Taking your anger out on the children after a hard day—the temptation to cruelty. Going out to eat when you can't afford it—the temptation to self-indulgence. Having a second helping and then a third—the temptation to gluttony. Firing off a hasty letter to a friend who hurt you—the temptation to revenge.

It's important to remember that the issue is not the particular temptation we face but how we respond to it. God is able to use even the worst temptation to bring us to the place where we will begin to grow spiritually. When Joseph ran away from Potiphar's wife (Genesis 39), he ended up in jail, but the whole experience produced in him the strength of character that prepared him to become the second most important ruler in Egypt. Lest we miss the point, let's remember that temptation itself is not evil; only the act of yielding is sinful. When we resist, we actually grow stronger.

Not long ago a friend commented that during a tense exchange with her teenage daughter, she "bit her tongue" instead of blowing her top. Every temptation—whether large or small—requires a moment-by-moment decision. When your boss asks you to fudge the figures on the monthly financial report, you only have a few seconds to decide how to respond. When you are surfing the Internet and happen to run across a site filled with pornography, you must choose immediately whether or not you'll click the mouse button. Sometimes you truly will have to bite your tongue, and then bite it again to keep from sinning.

When temptation comes knocking at your door, just say no.

Lord, give me the strength to say no when temptation knocks at my door today. Amen.

Name the greatest areas of temptation in your life. Which ones are currently giving you the greatest difficulty?

How has the Lord demonstrated His power to help you overcome a particular temptation?

THE TONGUE

Life and Death Are in Your Mouth!

The tongue has the power of life and death, and those who love it will eat its fruit.

Proverbs 18:21

Proverbs has a lot to say about what we say. In fact, the subject of the tongue and how we use our words is one of the major themes of this book. Over 150 times Proverbs refers to our lips, our mouth, and our tongue.

Words are important. After all, God created the universe with words. He spoke and it was so. Our Lord Jesus was called the Word: "In the beginning was the Word, and the Word was with God, and the Word was God. . . . The Word became flesh and made his dwelling among us" (John 1:1, 14).

"The tongue has the power of life and death, and those who love it will eat its fruit." Whether you know it or not, there is the power of life and there is the power of death within you. Everything you have said this week has either been life-giving or death-dealing, and there is nothing in between. The tongue has the power to kill, destroy, hurt, maim, and assassinate.

I read of a study released recently that states it takes eight to ten positive comments to offset one negative comment. In other words, eight to ten loving, caring, kind words are needed to eliminate the effects of just one hurtful word. Sometimes words that are spoken carelessly and viciously can never be erased from the blackboard of the mind.

The problem with words is that they can never be retrieved once they escape the mouth. The Bible describes the tongue as a world full of evil. From the tongue comes gossip, slander, hostility, cursing, and put-downs. We have all had times of regret or remorse when hurtful words have slipped out. Perhaps we spoke hastily to a co-worker, a neighbor, a classmate, a friend, a spouse, a parent, or a child. All of us have been eyewitnesses to the extreme damage the tongue can do.

One of my seminary professors often told us, "Men, it takes no size to criticize." I often think about that when I am tempted to take cheap shots at other people. The world is filled with critics; where are the affirmers? On every hand we have self-appointed "truth-tellers" whose calling in life seems to be finding what's wrong with everyone else. You know if you listen to them long enough they'll soon begin sniping at others.

But there is a better way. Years ago I picked up a copy of the Rotary Four-Way Test. It consists of four questions to ask yourself when you are tempted to say something unkind.

1. Is it the truth?
2. Is it fair to all concerned?
3. Will it build goodwill and better friendships?
4. Will it be beneficial to all concerned?

Pretty simple, isn't it? What a difference it would make if we would apply those four questions to every conversation this week.

Think about it. Every time you open your mouth, life or death comes out.

Lord, let Your life be in me so that I may speak words of life to all I meet. Amen.

How have you been hurt by the words of others? How have you hurt others with your own words? Are you better at criticizing or affirming?

Take a moment and ask God to help you speak only words of life today.

THOROUGHNESS

❖

Taking Care of Business

Be sure you know the condition of your flocks, give careful attention to your herds; for riches do not endure forever, and a crown is not secure for all generations. When the hay is removed and new growth appears and the grass from the hills is gathered in, the lambs will provide you with clothing, and the goats with the price of a field. You will have plenty of goats' milk to feed you and your family and to nourish your servant girls.

Proverbs 27:23–27

Some things in life are so simple as to defy any attempt to make them complicated. This passage brings before us one of those self-evident truths. *Take care of your business today and you will be in good shape tomorrow.* Simple, easy to understand. Focus on the task at hand, do it to the best of your ability, and don't worry about the future.

The reason is easy to understand. Since the future is always uncertain ("riches do not endure forever, and a crown is not secure"), the most you can do is to take care of business so you can tip the scales a bit in your favor. Even after you've done the best you can, some unexpected calamity may come, throwing your life into a tailspin. The best way to prepare for the unexpected is simply to be thorough in what you do today.

That leads to a profound insight: *99 percent of life is ordinary*. It's just the same old stuff day after day. You get up in the morning, take a shower, put your clothes on, eat breakfast, get the kids ready for school, go to work, hope the kids are OK, come back from work dead tired, read the paper, watch TV, try to be nice, eat supper, play with the kids, flop into bed dead tired, get up the next morning, and then do it all over again. That's the way life is.

Where do you begin in discovering the will of God? *You begin by doing what you already know to be the will of God in your present situation.* So many of us live for those high, mountain-peak experiences, for those times when the clouds part and God seems so close to us. If you are a student, the will of God is to do your homework. If you a lawyer, the will of God is to study the law. If you are a banker, the will of God is take care of the money entrusted to you. If you are a teacher, the will of God is to be prepared every time you step into your classroom.

The will of God always begins with the ordinary, the mundane, the usual. But that's a hard fact for a generation seeking something spectacular. Often when we say "God, show me Your will," what we really mean is, "Lord, give me some feeling, some insight, some spiritual revelation." And God says, "I have already shown you My will. Now just get up and do it!"

So many of us want to live only on the mountaintop. That's not where you discover God's will. *You discover God's will in the nitty-gritty of the valley every single day.* The Bible says, "Whatever your hand finds to do, do it with all your might" (Ecclesiastes 9:10). Why should God show you His will for the future if you aren't doing the will of God in the present?

Help me to be busy doing the work You have given me to do, O Lord. Save me from the folly of thinking that tomorrow is somehow more important than today. Amen.

How well have you been "taking care of business" lately?

Considering that "99 percent of life is ordinary," what is the will of God for you today?

What have you been putting off that needs to be done before you go to bed tonight?

THRIFT

***

How the Poor Become Rich

Dishonest money dwindles away, but he who gathers money little by little makes it grow.

Proverbs 13:11

This verse might be labeled "How to make money the old-fashioned way." Anything that comes too easily won't be greatly valued. That's one danger of giving a young person an inheritance too early in life (20:21). There is also a danger of running after some get-rich-quick scheme—the kind usually advertised in a late-night infomercial (28:20). But let a person toil and sweat to earn a paycheck and he will think twice before blowing it on some frivolous expenditure.

"Dishonest money dwindles away." According to the Bible, there are three legitimate ways to get money. First, you can work for it (2 Thessalonians 3:10). Second, you can make money through wise investments (Luke 19:11–27). Third, you can receive a gift or an inheritance (2 Corinthians 12:14). There is no fourth category, such as gambling.

Gambling is not work, for the gambler hopes to make money without working at all. Gambling is not an investment, for the gambler creates an artificial risk, hoping to make easy money. Gambling is not a gift, for the money is won from the losers, not given as a gift.

Why, then, do people gamble? They gamble because they think that with just a little bit of luck, they will win. And it doesn't matter whether the prize is ten dollars or ten thousand dollars, the motivating force is still the same. Gambling offers a shortcut, a way to get ahead quickly, a way to make some easy money.

Contrast that with the biblical principle of contentment. Consider Philippians 4:11*b*–13:

> I have learned to be content whatever the circumstances. I know what it is to be in need, and I know what it is to have plenty. I have learned the secret of being content in any and every situation, whether well fed or hungry, whether living in plenty or in want. I can do everything through him who gives me strength.

That last verse is often lifted out of the immediate context and used as a kind of spiritual pep pill. But taken in connection with the preceding verses, the meaning is that the Christian can find contentment in every situation through the power of the indwelling Christ.

Please understand. Contentment does not mean passive acceptance of a bad situation. It does not mean that I shouldn't try to better myself. Contentment is not the opposite of ambition. *But contentment does mean that if I find myself in a difficult position, I will thank God for the opportunity to trust Him, I will use every legitimate means to improve the situation, but I will not fall into the trap of trying to take shortcuts in order to find an easy way out.*

For those wishing to build their net worth, Solomon's advice is simple but very effective: "He who gathers money little by little makes it grow." This applies equally to savings or to investing. Take time, start small, work hard, learn the principles of investing, seek wise counsel, and most of all, don't throw your money away, either through greed, gullibility, or gambling.

In the fable of the tortoise and the hare, the tortoise won because he just kept plodding along. Be a tortoise and watch your money grow.

Lord, make me a tortoise when I am tempted to be a hare. Amen.

Have you ever gambled with your own money? If so, what happened?

What practical steps could you take to develop a thriftier lifestyle?

By nature are you more like the tortoise or the hare?

TOLERANCE

✦

A Misunderstood Virtue

A man's wisdom gives him patience; it is to his glory to overlook an offense.

Proverbs 19:11

The dictionary defines *tolerance* as "respecting the nature, beliefs, or behavior or others." To tolerate someone means to respect his opinion without necessarily agreeing with him. In that sense, tolerance is a noble virtue, for it allows us to live amicably with people who may be quite different from us. Indeed, without tolerance no society (or community or church or family, for that matter) could long endure.

Tolerance in the classical sense requires that we hold our convictions firmly while at the same time respecting those who may disagree. Sometimes tolerance will mean enduring foolish comments and overlooking offensive behavior by others.

But there is another, darker definition of tolerance emerging. Josh McDowell argues that toleration has replaced justice as the primary American virtue. *Tolerance today means that every view of truth and morality is equal to every other view.* This view of toleration differs from the classic view in that it says that there is no such thing as absolute truth. If you dare to tell someone else that what he is doing is wrong, you are going to be branded an intolerant bigot. In this view, everything is right and nothing is wrong. Some educators now argue that the public schools must teach students to be intolerant of intolerance. And who is the most intolerant of all in the eyes of the world? Christians are, because we believe in a Creator who established absolute standards of right and wrong. It may well be that in just a few years we will see a major cultural shift in which anyone who dares to speak out for God or against evil will risk being ostracized and publicly humiliated.

If that is true, then we will face some tough decisions in the days ahead. Satan's strategy has always been to stir up opposition to the church so that we will be intimidated into silence and compromise. It was true in the first century and it is still true today.

You may face opposition at work or from a critical colleague or from a classmate, a friend, a teacher, a neighbor, a relative, or even from your children or your spouse. Satan's primary strategy against the church is to discourage us by stirring up opposition so that we will stop spreading the Gospel.

In the years following World War II, the Quaker philosopher Elton Trueblood observed that America had become a "cut-flower" society where the bloom of Christian values had been cut off from its roots in the truth of God's Word. So much that passes for accepted truth is "accepted" simply because enough people have naively "accepted" it. But we as Christians do not determine our view of the world by reading the latest Gallup poll or by silently acquiescing to the views the majority currently happens to hold. As a matter of fact, the majority has usually been wrong throughout history, especially on matters of morality and spiritual truth.

Stand up for what you believe. Don't be intimidated by those who disagree, but don't be disagreeable either. Speak the truth, do it in love, and be patient with those who don't see things the way you do.

Lord Jesus, may I have Your perfect balance of grace and truth today. Amen.

What signs do you see of the "new" tolerance today? When does tolerance become compromise?

Where do you need to show more tolerance right now? Where do you need to stand up for what you believe?

TRIALS

❋

From Ashes to Gold

The crucible for silver and the furnace for gold, but the Lord tests the heart.

Proverbs 17:3

More than once lately I have had the opportunity to ponder why God allows some people to undergo prolonged disappointment. In one case, it is a prayer for a loved one that God has not answered, although the prayer has been offered again and again. In another case, it is a dream that seemed so close and then at the last second was snatched away. In another case, it is a broken friendship that cannot be repaired. In yet another case, it is a man in search of a job he cannot seem to find. In addition I have a good friend who has just been diagnosed with inoperable cancer.

What is the common thread? Why do the people of God suffer so many setbacks and difficulties? What lessons are we to learn from the disappointments we so often face?

Years ago I ran across a passage from the Old Testament that sheds light on this crucial question. Exodus 23 takes place at Mount Sinai just after God has given the Ten Commandments. Verses 27–28 describe what will happen as the Jews travel to the Promised Land: "I will send my terror ahead of you and throw into confusion every nation you encounter. I will make all your enemies turn their backs and run. I will send the hornet ahead of you to drive the Hivites, Canaanites and Hittites out of your way." That sounds good to me. If I'm an Israelite and I hear the Lord talking like that, I'm ready to march because it sounds like the trip to the Promised Land is going to be a piece of cake.

But that's not the whole story. Here are the next two verses: "But I will not drive them out in a single year, because the land would become desolate and the wild animals too numerous for you. Little by little I will drive them out before you, until you have increased enough to take possession of the land" (Exodus 23:29–30). Did you get that? God is promising ultimate victory, but He is also promising that it won't come quickly. Why? Because if victory comes quickly, the Israelites wouldn't be ready to handle it. Instead, He promises to work "little by little"—an inch here, a yard there, day by day leading His people and building their confidence in Him. Over time—and through many small battles—they will become strong enough to win the final victory.

That explains so much that happens to us. God works "little by little" to develop spiritual strength in us. If all our prayers were immediately answered, we'd soon take prayer for granted. We pray more, and we pray more fervently during a time of crisis because we know that if God doesn't help us, we're sunk.

When disappointment comes your way, keep four

truths fixed in your mind: (1) Today's disappointment is meant to prepare you for tomorrow's victory. (2) Tomorrow's victory will be sweeter because you had to fight harder to win it. (3) The Lord allows disappointment so that we will stay humble; He gives victory so that we will have hope. (4) He gives us just enough of each so that we might remember that, without His help, the Hivites would have wiped us out a long time ago.

Heavenly Father, in hard times I often do not know how to pray. May my trials lead me back to Your throne where I can find grace to help in the nick of time. Amen.

Name several occasions when God used disappointment to lead you to a deeper relationship with Him.

Could that be happening in some area of your life right now? Are you willing to trust God to finish His work at the right time and in the right way?

TRUST

❖

Learning to Lean on the Lord

Trust in the Lord with all your heart and lean not on your own understanding; in all your ways acknowledge him, and he will make your paths straight.

Proverbs 3:5–6

These two verses are among the most beloved in all the Bible. You may have memorized them in Sunday school when you were a child. Or perhaps you made a cross-stitch pattern of these words and hung it on your wall. Or you may have learned to sing these words as part of a contemporary worship chorus.

These words cling to the soul because they speak to a great need we all feel—the need for guidance. Proverbs 3:5–6 suggests the basis on which guidance will come. *It is a short course in knowing God's will for your life.* If you will learn what this passage is teaching and begin to apply it in your daily life, it will make a profound difference when you need to make a tough decision.

Not long ago I had a chance to study these verses for the first time. *As I did I discovered that six key words unlock the message of this text.* The word *trust* in Hebrew means "to lean with the full body," "to lay upon," "to rest the full weight upon." *To trust in the Lord is to rest your whole weight upon Him.*

To *lean* means to rest upon something for partial support. *Understanding* refers to the mental processes by which you analyze a problem, break it down into its smaller parts, and then make a decision about what you are going to do. To *acknowledge* means to know deeply *and* intimately. It's the kind of knowing that comes with personal experience. The words *make straight* picture a road that appears to be impassable. It winds through the mountains and down into the swamps. It seems to have a thousand switchbacks. Portions of the road are washed out, others are filled with potholes, still others are blocked by huge boulders. In some places the road apparently becomes a dead end.

It is the road of your life. As you look at it, it appears to be covered with boulders and rocks. Some parts of it seem to be filled with potholes; other sections appear to be going nowhere. That's the way life is.

Here is God's message to you from Proverbs 3:5–6. *If you will know God in every area of your life, He will take personal responsibility to make your way smooth and straight.* He will remove the obstacles if they need to be removed. He will fill in the potholes if they need to be filled. He will redirect the detour so that what seemed to be a dead end turns out to be the shortest way to reach your destination.

All you have to do is trust in the Lord. Lay yourself completely on Him for full support. Don't lean for support on your own human understanding. In all your ways know God intimately. He will take the path of your life—which seems to go up and down and around and sometimes seems to curve backwards—and will make your way straight. That's the promise of almighty God to you.

Lord, teach me to trust You even when I cannot see around the next bend in the road. Amen.

Name a time when God took the road of your life and "made your way straight."

What obstacles keep you from trusting God on a daily basis? What does it mean to know God deeply and intimately?

UNDERSTANDING

---※---

Learning from Your Mistakes

Understanding is a fountain of life to those who have it, but folly brings punishment to fools.

Proverbs 16:22

Some people never learn from their mistakes, which is why they repeat them. Others learn the first time and gain what Solomon calls "understanding." It is an inexhaustible fountain of practical truth that God gives to those who are good students of their own decisions. By contrast, fools never learn, and so God's discipline is wasted on them.

Here is a wonderful truth: *God can redeem your mistakes if you will let Him.* When Peter denied Jesus, the Lord never criticized him and never gave up on him. Jesus knew about Peter's denial long before it happened. He knew what Peter would do, He knew how he would react, and He knew the kind of man Peter would be afterward.

There is an important principle at work here. A bone that is broken often becomes stronger after it is healed. Something in the healing process actually makes the break point stronger than it was before. The same is true of a rope that breaks. In the hands of a master splicer, the rope once repaired will be stronger than it was before.

The same thing is true of our failures. God can take us where we are—broken—and can make us stronger than we were before. Though we fall and fall and fall, and though our faces are covered with the muck and grime of bitter defeat, by God's grace we can rise from the field of defeat to march on to new victory.

That's what happened to Peter. His guilt was turned into grace; his shame, into sympathy; his failure, into faithfulness.

Here is the proof: Peter did much more for Jesus Christ after his fall than he did before. Before his fall, he was loud, boisterous, and unreliable; afterward, he became a flaming preacher of the Gospel. Before, he was a big talker; afterward, he talked only of what Jesus Christ could do for others. He was the same man, but he was different. He was still Peter through and through, but he had been sifted by Satan, and in the sifting, the chaff of his life had been blown away.

When I pastored in Texas there was a woman in my church who called me often asking for spiritual help. I suppose over the course of five years we must have talked on the phone at least one hundred times. She stands out vividly in my mind because she always ended our conversations the same way. Whenever we came to the end of the call, Betty would always say, "Remember, Pastor Ray, we're only human."

That's a crucial insight for all of us less-than-perfect people. I often tell people that your past isn't nearly as important as where you are right now and where you plan to be tomorrow. Direction makes all the difference. We all stumble in many ways, and some of us fall hard because of our own stupidity. The wise man learns from his mistakes, gains understanding, and discovers that his failure has become a fountain of life to him. Only a fool keeps doing the same dumb thing over and over.

Lord God, I ask not for an easy road, but for new understanding of the path I should follow. Amen.

Can you think of a major mistake/sin/blunder that eventually became a "fountain of life" to you?

What lesson is God trying to teach you right now?

WAITING

✦

Give God Time to Work

Do not say, "I'll pay you back for this wrong!" Wait for the Lord, and he will deliver you.

Proverbs 20:22

One commentator notes that this verse is the answer to selfish haste. Often when we are mistreated we rush to get even with our tormentors, sometimes at the expense of our own reputation. But in our haste to balance the scales, we forget the words of Dr. Martin Luther King, Jr.: "The arm of the universe is long, but it bends toward justice."

Over and over Scripture exhorts us to "wait for the Lord." To us, *waiting* is nothing more than passive resignation, giving into our circumstances, throwing up our hands in despair and walking off the playing field. We don't "wait" for the Lord because we think that "waiting" means giving up.

But that only shows how little we understand either the Bible or the Lord. From a biblical perspective, waiting isn't passive; it's the most proactive thing we can do. To "wait" on the Lord means to get out of the way so that He can act. I would define waiting on the Lord this way: *It is being so confident in God that you refuse to take matters into your own hands.* When Jesus stood before His accusers, "He never said a mumblin' word." "When they hurled their insults at him, he did not retaliate; when he suffered, he made no threats. Instead, he entrusted himself to him who judges justly" (1 Peter 2:23). If you think it's easy to keep silent in the face of false accusations, it's only because you haven't tried it lately.

Nothing in life seems as hard to take as waiting. Maybe for a phone call or for a word from the doctor. Maybe for a job or for a letter you expected last week. Maybe for the fever to break or for someone you love to come home again.

People who spend time in the hospital understand this concept because hospital days don't last twenty-four hours; they last seventy-two hours. You look at the clock, thinking it has been five minutes and it has only been thirty seconds. Twenty minutes later it has only been three more minutes. This gives you plenty of time to think.

Perhaps an illustration will help. A few years ago a well-known football coach, upon being fired, commented that "Scripture says, 'This too shall pass.'" He was partly right and partly wrong. Scripture nowhere says, "This too shall pass." The phrase comes from an old tale about an Oriental monarch who asked his wise men to come up with a sentence that would suit every occasion, good or bad. Abraham Lincoln once repeated the story and then added this comment concerning "This too shall pass": "How much it expresses! How chastening in the hour of pride! How consoling in the depths of affliction!"

If "this too shall pass" doesn't come from the Bible, the thought is entirely biblical. The good times and the bad times, the joys and the sorrows, the Super Bowl victories and the untimely firings—these will all eventually pass away.

Take heart while you wait on the Lord. Though for the present you are sorely mistreated, this too shall pass. In the meantime, let God be God and give Him room to work.

Lord, when I am tempted to interfere, please remind me that You don't need any help from me. Amen.

What are you waiting for right now? In what areas of life are you tempted to "help God out"?

Why is the phrase "This too shall pass" both chastening and consoling?

WISDOM

✦

The Art of Skillful Living

Wisdom is supreme; therefore get wisdom. Though it cost all you have, get understanding. Esteem her, and she will exalt you; embrace her, and she will honor you. She will set a garland of grace on your head and present you with a crown of splendor.

Proverbs 4:7–9

The Hebrew word for wisdom refers to much more than an accumulation of facts. In the Old Testament this word was used for anyone who had an unusual degree of skill in a given area. For instance, if a potter could create beautiful tableware, he was said to have wisdom. The same thing would be said of a composer who could take notes and put them together to make beautiful music. A gifted speaker who knew how to use words to move people was called wise by those who heard him. The word means to be skilled in some area of life. Wisdom in the book of Proverbs might be defined as the ability to live life skillfully from God's point of view. It comes from viewing life from a vertical perspective and acting accordingly.

That's why the first step in acquiring wisdom is simply to desire it more than anything else. Like everything else in the spiritual realm, wisdom is free for the asking, but it will cost you all you have. Because it is supreme among the virtues, it cannot be had at a bargain basement price. Let no man think he will become wise by accident. No such thing has ever happened since the beginning of creation. No, a man must search after wisdom as if he were searching for silver or gold; he must set aside trivial pursuits in favor of that which comes only from God.

You must turn from evil if you truly want wisdom. In one place we are told that "the fear of the Lord is the beginning of wisdom" (9:10); in another, that to fear the Lord means hating evil (8:13). You can live in the darkness or you can walk in the light, but you cannot do both at the same time. God invites you to a brand-new life. Do you want wisdom? Then "come . . . eat . . . drink . . . leave . . . walk" (9:5–6). You can have it if you want it, but you must make the decision and pursue wisdom with all your heart.

But there is a further step you must take. It involves humbling yourself, admitting your need, confessing your lack, and asking God to help you. Several times Solomon warns against the man who is "wise in his own eyes" (26:12; 28:11). If you think you have arrived—well, you're right, for with that attitude, you aren't going to go any further with the Lord.

After his retirement, someone asked Charlie Riggs the secret of his success in overseeing follow-up and new believer discipleship for the Billy Graham organization. "Every day I always prayed, 'Lord, put me in over my head.' That way I knew if the Lord didn't help me, I was sunk," he replied. Solomon would heartily approve.

If you want wisdom, you can have it. It's free, but it will cost you all you have.

Lord, I seek Your wisdom—nothing more, nothing less, nothing else. Amen.

In what areas of your life do you need God's wisdom? What do you think it will cost you to get it?